COLD★WAR
ILLINOIS

COLD ★ WAR ILLINOIS

CHRISTOPHER STURDEVANT

THE
History
PRESS

Published by The History Press
Charleston, SC
www.historypress.com

Images in public domain unless otherwise noted.

First published 2020

Manufactured in the United States

ISBN 9781467145022

Library of Congress Control Number: 2020932083

Notice: The information in this book is true and complete to the best of our knowledge. It is offered without guarantee on the part of the author or The History Press. The author and The History Press disclaim all liability in connection with the use of this book.

CONTENTS

PREFACE

As a follow-up to *Cold War Wisconsin* in 2018, I turned my attention south of the border to the great state of Illinois, known as the Prairie State or, more popularly, as the Land of Lincoln. The era was a curious time, as Illinois was connected to America's longest and costliest conflict during the twentieth century. Some of these connections were very personal, as I had met extraordinary people such as Werner Juretzko of Mount Prospect, a G-2 intelligence agent who served prison time in East German Stasi prisons from 1955 to 1961. From others, like Wesley Adamczyk of Chicago, I learned a great deal of the hardships of Polish citizens as they were deported by Joseph Stalin after the Soviet Union invaded that country. The Molotov–Von Ribbentrop pact signed by Nazi Germany and the USSR in September 1939 violently split Poland between the signatories. The Polish experience would serve as a model of war in other otherwise peaceful European countries as the Second World War unfolded. Both of these larger-than-life men knew the horrors of war and of communism in particular, an ideology that was overshadowed by Nazism but bred brutal dictatorships that untold millions all over the globe suffered from immensely.

Generations have passed since these individuals and countless others experienced the firsthand horrors felt by millions of citizens caught behind the Iron Curtain in European countries. The Eastern and Central Europeans were told of their "liberation" from the Soviets only to find constant lies, surveillance, limited freedoms and destitution. Witnessing young people embrace fragments of socialism has, as of this writing, caused great consternation, as these citizens increasingly accept the premise of a "just" society based on "equality" promised under such socialist systems. Past experience has proven exactly how horrible and unjust those societies flirting with such idealistic fantasy became, as those conquered could attest.

In my formative years during the 1980s, Ronald Reagan was a beacon of optimism and, in real time, an embodiment of much of what the Cold War came to signify from the American perspective. He single-handedly changed the nature of relations with the Soviet Union, upending conventional wisdom by ditching the stale policies of "detente," or getting along and accepting such evil systems, by hammering them at every turn. Reagan would go on to become the face of victory in the Cold War, despite his contemporaries in the political class of Washington, D.C., dismissing his policies as foolish and dangerous. Instinctively, Reagan was correct that the Soviets were weak, outside of their military prowess and reliance on nuclear weapons. The world needed somebody to fight back against the Soviets, and America under Ronald Reagan answered the call. The fall of the Berlin Wall in 1989, along with the Chernobyl accident in Ukraine in 1986, became just two of a series of events signifying the end of communist rule. For a brief moment, a celebration of the end of tyranny in Europe ensued.

This book will trace these and other individuals and events of significance during the Cold War from a local Illinois perspective, turning the Cold War inside out to view it separately from those events occurring in the corridors of Washington, D.C., and those halfway around the globe. The Space Race, the Arms Race, Fidel Castro's Cuban revolution, the Peace Movement and significant players with Illinois connections factor heavily in the story of the Cold War.

A COLD WAR PRIMER

WHAT WAS THE COLD WAR ANYWAY?

Entire tomes have been written on the topic of the Cold War, but very few have been written about the local aspects of the conflict. Most accounts are military in nature, written about leaders in power during the Cold War, various flashpoints and a focus on the larger picture of Soviet-U.S. relations. The term "Cold War" was applied to this grandstanding between the heavyweights of the United States and the Soviet Union by either Bernard Baruch or Orson Welles—it is subject to debate but was nonetheless a sobering reality after years of turmoil during the Second World War. Having been removed from the era for so long, however, the term "Cold War" has sown confusion to those not born of the era, having no context of America's longest and costliest conflict in history.

Decades after the Berlin Wall fell in 1989, the Cold War seemed to vanish quickly from the minds of most Americans in the United States. The era was subsequently underappreciated and largely unknown to more recent generations, glossed over in historical education for decades. The American public, largely sheltered from the conflict abroad, quickly turned its attention from the crumbling workers' paradise in the Soviet Union to the conflicts in the Middle East that would become a fixture in American foreign policy for decades thereafter—first Operation Desert Shield/Desert Storm in Iraq and then events in Afghanistan and Iraq after the 9/11 attacks, along with regional skirmishes in Syria and with Iran, among others.

BEGINNINGS

As history comes more into focus, we can now view the Cold War era as a large period of the twentieth century, dating back to the First World War and the rise of the early Soviets. The Bolshevik revolutionaries were a driving force in ousting Czar Nicholas II from Russia and, subsequently, the provisional government set up in Russia after the czar's ouster in 1917. Deep suspicion of the communism espoused by these revolutionaries—a bizarre ideology that included abolishing private property and religion and other basic human rights—resulted in immediate derision by many in the West. Embargoes began, followed by warfare with the Russian Bolsheviks, pursued under the guise of solidifying the Eastern Front against the kaiser's German armies.

The First World War continued after Russia's withdrawal and was a pretext of the Allied Expeditionary Force landing in North Russia and Siberia. Woodrow Wilson authorized more than thirteen thousand American troops to join Winston Churchill's initiative to send British and Commonwealth troops to intervene in the port cities of Archangel and Murmansk to the north, as well as the port city of Vladivostok in eastern Siberia. These troops aligned themselves loosely with the White armies in the quest to crush the Bolsheviks in their infancy during the Russian Civil War. Soldiers from Illinois would be sent to these front lines instead of France, where the center of the fighting continued to rage.

Once the Armistice was signed in November 1918, questions arose as to why these men remained in Russia. Arctic sea ice wouldn't melt until the spring of 1919, and in the meantime, American troops would skirmish with Bolsheviks along rail and river routes in the vast forests of North Russia. Pressure built to bring the boys home from this alien landscape in these brutally cold and snowy faraway lands. After the Western powers finally withdrew, the Soviets—under Lenin, Stalin and others going forward—would propagandize these "imperialists." The intervention was a gamble by Churchill that didn't pay off, and as a result, the Cold War fight would last a long seventy-three years, until the Soviet Union finally dissolved in 1991. Today, many of the "Polar Bears" who fought and died in North Russia are buried near Detroit, Michigan, commemorating a Cold War beginning.

THE MODERN COLD WAR

As the Second World War—a pause in souring Soviet-U.S. relations to focus on a common enemy, the German Third Reich—came to a close, the modern Cold War was ushered in quickly. The Cold War would reignite between the two remaining superpowers after the conflict concluded in 1945, when Soviet troops remained in Eastern and Central Europe. The Soviets promised elections after the war's conclusion, but these were nothing more than puppet governments that went unopposed for much of the latter half of the twentieth century. A military buildup (the Arms Race) between the Soviet Union and the West, led by the United States of America, was an inevitable outcome from this fragile alliance with the common enemy of Nazi Germany and would shape postwar boundaries and spheres of influence, especially in Europe. Nuclear war was the new reality of the postwar era, a dangerous byproduct of using atomic weapons on Japan to end the Pacific War in 1945. The Cold War conflict was seen as a competition in the sciences, education, culture, athletics, exploration and even right down to family life—competing philosophies of capitalism and communism, freedom and restriction, individualism and collectivism. No country or region was untouched; the Cold War found its way into everything and everywhere, including into the Arctic and Antarctic lands north and south. Thankfully, this undeclared war never resulted in a direct third world conflict in the twentieth century.

Thus, anchored by these two superpowers and their respective allies, the Cold War progressed; the United States and the Soviet Union stood toe to toe for forty-six years, waiting for the other side to blink and stand down. Since the first atomic bomb was tested and used to end the Second World War in 1945, both superpowers raced to yield more destructive weapons to outdo each other. What ensued was the threat and fear of nuclear war for decades during the Cold War, and it still worries the world today. Both the United States and the Soviet Union set out to dominate land, air, sea and space, as those arenas would become the focus of outmaneuvering the other side. Alliances were formed in both the East and the West. On behalf of the West, the North Atlantic Treaty Organization (NATO) would be formed in 1949, forging itself in case of the very real possibility of Soviet attack. In response, the communists took hold of Eastern and Central Europe, forming the Warsaw Pact in 1955.

FIRST CONFLICT

A conflict over the status of Berlin broke out when the Soviets blockaded routes to the city in 1948. Like Germany itself, the city of Berlin had also been divided between East and West Berlin, with Soviet control over East Berlin and Allied control over West Berlin (French, British and American sectors consolidated). Deep inside what became East Germany in 1949, Berlin was surrounded by hostility. Soviet leader Joseph Stalin was determined to choke the city off from the Allies and force the Western powers out of Berlin. Through a treaty at the Yalta Conference in 1945, the West had access to the Allied sector through roads and air corridors. With memories of the Second World War fresh in American minds, war was to be avoided at all costs. Harry Truman decided to keep the citizens of West Berlin alive through the air, and the Berlin Airlift was born. For nearly one year, West Berliners were supplied with fuel, coal, medicines, foodstuffs and other supplies. Crisis was averted. Although the United States would not abandon West Berlin and its citizens, the Cold War was well underway.

Of course, the context of the Cold War is long gone, having been left to books about various historical events of the twentieth century and artifact relics in museums. It was an era when record players and rotary phones were high tech, James Bond worked covertly to stop the villains, and being a superhero meant something like Superman's "peace, justice and the American way." The lexicon and symbols of the Cold War, not surprisingly, have changed as well. There is no Berlin Wall surrounding that city and no longer an Iron Curtain across Eastern and Central Europe. Also absent are the high-level summits that took place, with the chattering class in Washington, D.C., talking up a peaceful approach to solving the Cold War—a gamesmanship where the ruling classes of each country protected their own. Nike today is a shoe company. Few would confuse that Nike with nuclear-equipped missile systems deployed around the United States to shoot down long-range Soviet bombers.

The Cold War's importance should not be underestimated, as it overshadowed and shaped our entire American way of life in the twentieth century and beyond. Militaries were sustained, diplomacy undertaken, foreign aid given to rebuild and sustain countries, weapons systems developed and even a national highway system built in the United States. Preservation efforts and attention to this fascinating era are underrepresented, and proper recognition to the many millions of Cold War veterans has been lacking. Writing this book is a first step with that need in mind, especially telling the important local story of the Cold War.

Contrary to popular belief, the Cold War era was anything but "peaceful." Nuclear war was the penultimate outcome, a certain Armageddon that could destroy humanity. The Cold War was truly a world war, fought and challenged across the globe. Due to ever-increasing needs for information on the other side, the United States sent many dangerous missions behind the Iron Curtain. American planes were shot down over Eastern Europe, for example. Many men are still listed as Missing in Action from missions setting out to test response of Warsaw Pact radar systems. The Cold War was dangerous and deadly, fraught with conflicts from Asia to Africa, Korea, Vietnam and Angola.

WHAT HAPPENED TO THE COLD WAR?

Studying history brought out a fascination with the Cold War era that formed my childhood, an era that simply disappeared after the fall of the Berlin Wall in 1989. Two years later, the Cold War whimpered to a close with the subsequent dissolution of the Soviet Union in 1991. Even Ronald Reagan, arguably the one who took it to the Soviets rather than trying to make peaceful coexistence with socialism, was surprised that it occurred so quickly. Yet with all of the effort, money, politicking and influence for this forty-six-year conflict, no ticker-tape parades took place. The Kremlin recalled its spies abroad and gave them medals. Yet in America, there were no large-scale celebrations in the streets like with the end of the Second World War. Likewise, no Nuremberg Trials like those convened after the Second World War for war crimes on the defunct Soviet Union and its Warsaw Pact alliance. The reunification of Germany went so quickly that legal terminology allowed secret police such as the East German Stasi off the hook for its crimes against its own citizenry. As a whole, time simply kept marching along, as if the Cold War never really occurred here in the United States.

REMINISCING: A COLD WAR CHILDHOOD

As a curious child of the Cold War era, I grew of age in the 1980s reading newspapers, magazines and countless atlases while studying the world. Current events, history, math and geography were of high interest. If not for being active playing sports, both in the neighborhood and at school, I likely would have been the most uninteresting kid around due to my interest in these topics. And as I continued to be exposed to developments of the day, few people around me seemed to have either the interest in or answers to questions percolating in my young brain. It was up to me to find out and put the pieces together. My passions were stoked at a young age and would follow me well into adulthood. Little was I aware that my search into the Cold War would take me to places such as North Korea, Chernobyl and Afghanistan in the twenty-first century.

The Cold War was certainly nowhere to be found while I was growing up in Janesville, Wisconsin. My hometown, near the Illinois border, was seemingly as far away as possible from any direct involvement in covert operations around the world, let alone diplomatic circles that dominated foreign policy in Washington, D.C., and elsewhere. The highlight around Janesville, as I recall, was hearing abundant rumors that a local company called the Accudyne Corporation was housing nuclear material. It turned out, many years later, that this assessment was correct and that there were other secret storage facilities in southern Wisconsin.

By far the largest influence on the population was Hollywood. We watched movies such as *Red Dawn*, *Damnation Alley*, the James Bond films and, of course, *Rocky IV*, where Rocky Balboa takes on the Soviet Ivan Drago inside Russia. These movies convinced us of America's superiority to communism, as well as its ability to adapt and survive war/nuclear war with the Soviet Union and its proxies. Teenagers in *Red Dawn*, portrayed by the likes of Patrick Swayze and Charlie Sheen, were responsible for teaching the Cuban armies and Soviet military advisers that a war with America was never going to end well for them. These characters connected with Americans of all ages while sharing a Hollywood fixation on the apocalypse, misery and teamwork to overcome the odds as Americans.

Curiously, there were no similar movies created in the Soviet Union. To have such a notion of American power was off limits. A visit to the Chernobyl nuclear exclusion zone in 2016 shed some light for me on how the Soviet military viewed the United States. Outside of Pripyat, the city that housed the workers at the Chernobyl nuclear plants, I was part of a small tour group visiting a top-secret radar base called Chernobyl-2. During the base's active time in the Soviet era, only those with a need-to-know clearance were aware of its existence. Its mission was to detect United States and NATO activities such as aircraft, bombers, space and satellite launches and missiles. The detection source used was a one-thousand-foot-wide, four-hundred-foot-tall DUGA (ARCH) Radar system. When the Chernobyl disaster struck, the base was abandoned. The radar base now lies in ruins, like other uninhabited areas in the nuclear exclusion zone.

On the walls of base buildings were murals and guides depicting Americans as cowboys, with some soldiers using reckless flamethrowers. The Soviet military had the impression that everyone in America owned a gun and acted like John Wayne. As a matter of fact, several former Soviet military personnel over the years stated to me that it was believed an invasion on American soil would have created an enormous number of casualties due to this view. As the Soviet perspective demonstrated, an armed civilian populace was influential in deterring a mighty foreign military foe.

On a larger scale, from my view as a child, I recognized that the dominant foreign policy in the late 1970s clearly concerned the Soviet Union and the Iron Curtain countries. That geographic and political reality grabbed my attention during the boycott of the Winter Olympics in 1980, when the United States defeated the Soviets in the hockey semifinals, dubbed the "Miracle on Ice." In 2012, some thirty years after the fact, I found myself traveling in Finland, where a fellow Rotary member in Jyvaskyla reminded me, in a jocular fashion, that the United States defeating Finland in 1980 for the gold medal was "not forgotten." The unbelievable showing in hockey was followed soon after by an American boycott of the Moscow Summer Olympics, due to the Soviet invasion of Afghanistan. In 1984, the Soviet Union would return the favor and boycott the Summer Olympics in Los Angeles. Warsaw Pact countries followed suit, minus Romania, which competed in Los Angeles despite pressure from the Soviet Union.

Images from Moscow beamed through television screen in the 1980s, and as depicted on television and the news, Moscow was clearly a dreaded place by all standards, based on gray, stoic and lifeless people in a barren, cold landscape illustrated daily. Long lines for consumer goods were a fact of life for Russians, I presumed. I would later learn that this was partially due to no use of preservatives for bread, which would go stale quickly. Others from the Communist Bloc would share stories with me while waiting in line. Many individuals over the years stated that, as children, waiting in line was considered a social time among neighbors and acquaintances. Hours later, the families and friends would come up empty-handed despite their rations cards, only to awake early the following day to stand in line once again. This contrasted sharply with my observances despite growing up in a poor family. I could still shop at stores with ample selection of foods, with several stores a simple walk or drive down the road from where I lived. Reliable vehicles were readily attainable for a few hundred dollars growing up, unlike in communist countries, which had waiting lists for vehicles that were made of cotton composite materials. Thus, at a young age, I could grasp that there was something different between our two countries.

WHAT ARE THOSE SOVIETS UP TO?

In the early 1980s, Soviet leaders were falling over like dominoes. The old guard after Nikita Khrushchev continued its power grip over the Soviet Union. These reliable and connected members had demonstrated their commitment to the Soviet state for decades and would continue to rule. First Leonid Brezhnev in 1982, followed by Yuri Andropov in 1984 and then another former KGB head, Konstantin Chernenko, in 1985 before Mikhail Gorbachev assumed power. I scratched my head, wondering why these leaders kept dying off. In retrospect, President Ronald Reagan was asked by the press why more summits with the Soviets didn't occur. Reagan responded that he wanted to, but they kept dying on him.

The Soviets made clear who was in charge of Poland during my formative years. One of the most distinct memories I had as a nine-year-old was reading about a place in Europe called Poland. As I became more fascinated about this geopolitical world, I read about martial law being imposed on civilians by that country's military leader and wondered what was going on. Why would people in these cities be under a curfew? As a young boy, I had a curfew, but it was imposed by my mother and not a military general.

That episode of history involved a movement called Solidarity, which had been taking place in the shipyards of Gdansk, Poland, since the 1970s. Protests broke out over rations, wages, housing and jobs. Dissidents, protesters and those merely aiding the opposition and Solidarity movement were arrested and detained, and the Soviets threatened to move into Poland unless the communist-backed Polish government did something about it. The events in Poland in 1981 would form the basis of my Cold War interest many years later. Lech Wałęsa, one of the principal leaders of the Solidarity movement, would eventually become president of Poland in 1990 after the fall of the Berlin Wall. With some exceptions (notably Nicolae and Elena Ceaușescu in Romania), peaceful revolutions would break the Soviet grasp of most Iron Curtain countries and some Soviet republics. The story of the Polish people is a remarkable one, and the Soviet treatment of Poles who eventually arrived in Illinois will be a topic in this book.

THE RISE OF RONALD REAGAN

Growing up during the 1980s allowed me to bear witness to Ronald Reagan's presidential tenure, and his tough talk about the Soviets was always in the spotlight. Reagan, as highlighted in this book, diverted from prior American policies and directly challenged the Soviet Union and its existence. Soviet and communist ideology clearly dehumanized populations in their sphere of influence, and the Soviet military state was a constant threat to its neighbors while also meddling on every continent. There wasn't a day that went by as Reagan took it to the Soviets. His talk of the Evil Empire and proposing a Strategic Defense Initiative in 1983, a program that would create technology to shoot down incoming nuclear missiles, sparked not only my own imagination but also the nation's. Laser weapons (à la "Star Wars") were derided by the press yet caught the imagination of those enjoying that blockbuster. Reagan visited the Soviet Union in 1987, and in a wholly coincidental moment, a photo purportedly exists of him shaking hands with one Vladimir Putin in Red Square during his visit. Earlier that year, when standing near the Brandenburg Gate adjacent to the Berlin Wall, Reagan asked Mr. Gorbachev to "tear down this wall!" To many people's amazement, it fell in 1989. I could only bear witness to the event on a television screen. The Soviet Union sat motionless and did not invade with tanks, unlike in decades past, as nations behind the Iron Curtain one by one claimed their own sovereignty. The Soviet Union would dissolve in 1991. Shortly thereafter, George H.W. Bush was signing the Strategic Arms Reduction Treaty and giving a televised speech to the Polish Duma in 1991. What started my fascination with Poland from 1981 gave rise to the beginning of a post–Cold War world. In many respects, we are still living in one today.

WHAT THIS BOOK IS ABOUT

When confronted with the idea of undertaking Cold War education and preservation efforts, I asked two distinct questions. First, what were the origins of the Cold War? Secondly, what was the local impact? Geographically speaking, the United States was far away from the events unfolding around the rest of the world after the Second World War. Besides those serving in the armed forces, those with relatives in those areas of the world—especially in such places as Europe, Asia or Latin America—were among those more attuned to the era. Likewise, spending extended time abroad allowed many Americans to experience the Soviet Union and the Warsaw Pact countries as they offered a glimpse into life behind the Iron Curtain. On the whole, however, as Americans we too often thought of the Cold War as ephemeral or occurring somewhere else: Berlin, Cuba, Vietnam, Korea and so on. But where did the men and women who served in the U.S. armed forces come from? Where did Cold War munitions, trucks, ships and other war support initiate from? How about our politicians, diplomats and others who would figure so prominently in many Cold War events?

After all, it was Ronald Reagan, the boy from Tampico, challenging the Soviets as president in Washington, D.C. Ernest Hemingway of the Chicago suburb of Oak Brook captured the imagination of the world with his writing and exploits in the Spanish Civil War and residence in Cuba. The Rock Island Arsenal and Joliet Army Ammunition Plants were manufacturing artillery, propellants and even rockets to support our troops in wartime, and Nike Hercules nuclear-equipped missiles in Chicago/Northwest Indiana were deterring a Soviet bomber invasion in Illinois. Each of these Cold War entities had local connotations. Notably, our military personnel and politicians came from somewhere, and defense plants employed workers who made war materiel someplace.

Thus, Illinois was at the forefront of the Cold War. The state played host to military bases, producing armaments and defending American territory from enemy attack. In addition, there were countless notable personalities, such as President Reagan, that would define the twentieth-century experience. Twenty Nike surface-to-air missile systems were deployed in the Chicago/Northwest Indiana area, scanning the skies for Soviet long-range nuclear bombers. Walt Disney and Bobby Fischer, an unlikely Cold Warrior in the chess world, were born in the Windy City. The Great Lakes Naval Base, along with Scott and Canute Air Force Bases, played a critical role in training and maintaining a military presence in the state, readying a fight for a third world war that thankfully never occurred. The Rock Island Arsenal was host to producing small arms and howitzers and even developing an atomic cannon. Servicemen from the upper Midwest were even sent to the Russian front during World War I, fighting the early Bolsheviks and the Red Army during the Russian Civil War in 1919. Tying these events and personalities together is a challenging task—a jigsaw puzzle.

This book is meant to be a thought-provoking look at the Cold War heritage in Illinois, examining ties to the larger struggle between the United States and the Soviet Union. It is not meant to be a definitive work, as it is often written in an anecdotal tone, picking up stories from a patchwork of friends and acquaintances who have been invaluable during their own experiences in the Cold War era. In some cases, these stories are unknown and have not been told until now, especially in context with the plethora of Cold War history occurring right here in the Midwest. Sprinkled into this tale of Cold War Illinois are personal observances from travels abroad into the legacies of the Cold War in places such as North Korea, Chernobyl and Afghanistan, where relevant. The Cold War lives on if we know where to look. Above all, I sincerely hope that you, the reader, will find this work enjoyable and interesting, perhaps even recalling this captivating history for those who lived through the latter part of the twentieth century.

Special thanks go out to Ben Gibson of The History Press for the opportunity to write this book. Gratitude to my project editor, Ryan Finn, as well as marketing and sales staff. Tremendous thanks to friends, family, co-workers and Cold War colleagues such as Cold War spy Werner Juretzko, Wesley Adamczyk (survivor of the forced Soviet journey to Siberia), North Korean POW Richard Rogala and many others for their support throughout this endeavor.

CHAPTER 1

RADICALS

COMMUNISTS BURIED AT FOREST PARK CEMETERY

C hicago has long been associated with outspoken leaders regarding social justice, equality, workplace issues and civil rights. Oftentimes these protest movements are peaceful protests against government policies or movements to apply pressure to change laws. On the opposite side of the scale, however, is outright force through direct action, intimidation and violence that targets people and property to achieve a certain goal. The leaders and select movements in this book comprise dissidents and events in relation to the Cold War and its roots in Marxist-Leninist thought. As a matter of fact, the Forest Home Cemetery in Forest Park, Illinois, laid to rest several notable social dissidents, anarchists, Bolsheviks and other communists dating back into the nineteenth century.

The latter part of that century saw a rise in labor organizations dedicated to change in working conditions, wages, safety and workday length, with the Haymarket Affair in 1886 becoming an early flashpoint and a symbol of Chicago's involvement. That trend would continue into the twentieth century as Marxist-Leninist tendencies took over segments of the labor movement, inspired by the Bolshevik takeover of Russia and the creation of the Soviet Union into the 1920s. The Second World War, along with revelations that Soviet leader Joseph Stalin conspired with Adolf Hitler to divide Poland in September 1939, tempered American communist and socialist ties to the Soviet Union. The rise of the counterculture and the New Left during the postwar years would evolve into a generational divide in the 1960s. Although demonstrators were largely peaceful, those turning violent were induced by the likes of Students for a Democratic Society

(SDS), which involved two principal leaders from Chicago, Bill Ayers and Bernardine Dohrn. Continuing the tradition of the Haymarket martyrs in the nineteenth century, the Weathermen and Weather Underground would continue opposing American involvement in the Vietnam War, as well as social justice concerns into the 1970s.

CHICAGO RED SQUAD

Red Squad units with police departments were not specific to Chicago in particular, but a case against using unwarranted surveillance methods was brought by the American Civil Liberties Union (ACLU) and the Alliance to End Repression in 1974.

According to the Encyclopedia of Chicago, the arm of Chicago's law enforcement known alternately as the Industrial Unit, the Intelligence Division, the Radical Squad or the Red Squad had its roots in the Gilded Age, when class conflict encouraged employers to ally themselves with Chicago's police against the city's increasingly politicized workforce. Following the Haymarket bombing, Captain Michael J. Schaack orchestrated a vicious campaign against anarchism, resulting in 260 arrests, bribed witnesses, attacks on immigrants and labor activists and convoluted theories of revolutionary conspiracy. Continuing its use of both overt and covert tactics—such as surveillance, infiltration and intimidation—Chicago's Red Squad in the 1920s under Make Mills shifted its attention from anarchists to individuals and organizations whom the Red Squad believed to be communist. Casting a wide net, the squad by 1960 had collected information on approximately 117,000 Chicagoans, 141,000 out-of-towners and 14,000 organizations. After the 1968 Democratic National Convention, the Red Squad expanded its targets from radical organizations like the Communist and Socialist Workers Parties to minority and reform organizations, including the American Civil Liberties Union, National Association for the Advancement of Colored People, National Lawyers Guild and Operation PUSH.

After eleven years of litigation, a 1985 court decision ended the Chicago Police Department's Subversive Activities Unit's unlawful surveillance of political dissenters and their organizations. In the fall of 1974, the Red Squad destroyed 105,000 individual and 1,300 organizational files when it learned that the Alliance to End Repression was filing a lawsuit against the unit for violating the U.S. Constitution.[1]

FOREST HOME CEMETERY, FOREST PARK, ILLINOIS

A who's who list of revolutionaries, socialists, anarchists and communists of the early Bolshevik persuasion can be found at a cemetery in the suburbs of Chicago. These individuals believed in communism as a form of governance in the United States. According to the Encyclopedia Britannica, communism is a political and economic doctrine that aims to replace private property and a profit-based economy with public ownership and communal control of at least the major means of production (e.g., mines, mills and factories) and the natural resources of a society. Communism is thus a form of socialism—a higher and more advanced form, according to its advocates.[2]

A monument is dedicated to those who perished in the incident at Haymarket Square. As various speakers were advocating an eight-hour workday and addressing other grievances to a large crowd, a bomb was thrown into the mass of people gathered around to listen. Police clashes ensued, and the origins of the Red Squad took root. Of those revolutionaries interred at the Forest Home Cemetery, two have partially buried remains in the Kremlin Wall in Moscow, owing their service to the building of the Soviet revolution abroad.

William "Big Bill" Haywood

William Haywood rose to such prominence as labor adviser to Lenin's Bolshevik government in 1921. Half of his ashes are buried in the Kremlin in Moscow, one of three Americans to hold such distinction—the others being John Reed (author of *Ten Days that Shook the World*) and Communist Party USA founder Charles Ruthenberg.

William Haywood signed up to become a Western Federation of Mining (WFM) member while working in a silver mine in Idaho in 1895, thus formally beginning his involvement in America's labor movement. Haywood immediately became active in the WFM, and by 1900, he had become a member of the national union's General Executive Board. Haywood was falsely implicated in a bombing murder of Idaho governor Frank Steunenburg in 1905. After being acquitted in the trial in 1907, Haywood became a celebrity in the unionized world and became active in the Socialist Party soon thereafter. He would take an active interest in organizing strikes at textiles mills in Massachusetts and New York and began to socialize with other progressive circles.

William "Big Bill" Haywood.

Haywood's run of freedom would be short-lived. The Espionage Act of 1917 became a precursor to raiding Industrial Workers of the World (IWW) meetings across the country. With the approval of President Woodrow Wilson, the Justice Department proceeded to arrest 165 IWW members for "conspiring to hinder the draft, encourage desertion, and intimidate others in connection with labor disputes." In April 1918, Haywood was put on trial for five months, a record at that time. He remained free on bail while on appeal, and in 1921, after appeal efforts were exhausted, Haywood skipped out on a $15,000 bail and fled to the Soviet Union. It was there he would become a labor adviser to Lenin's Bolshevik government until 1923. In 1928, Haywood died in his Moscow apartment. Half of his ashes were buried in the Kremlin wall; an urn containing the other half of his ashes was sent to Chicago and buried near the Haymarket Martyrs' Monument.

Elizabeth Gurley Flynn

A founding member of the American Civil Liberties Union in 1920, Flynn played a leading role in the campaign against the convictions of Sacco and Vanzetti. Flynn was particularly concerned with women's rights, such as supporting birth control and women's suffrage. Flynn also criticized the leadership of trade unions for being male-dominated and not reflecting the needs of women.

Flynn became national chairwoman of the Communist Party of the United States in 1961. She made several visits to the Soviet Union and died while there on September 5, 1964, at seventy-four. The Soviet government gave her a state funeral in Red Square, with more than twenty-five thousand people attending. In accordance with her wishes, Flynn's remains were flown to the United States for burial at Chicago's Waldheim Cemetery near the graves of Eugene Dennis, Bill Haywood, Emma Goldman and the other Haymarket Riot martyrs.

William Z. Foster

William Foster was a committed Stalinist and head of the Communist Party USA in the 1920s. Originally a Socialist Party member and labor organizer in the early part of the twentieth century, Foster joined the Communist Party after the First World War. He began his close relationship to the Soviet Union after being invited by future Communist Party USA leader Earl Browder to attend a conference in Moscow in 1921. Foster was appointed as agent of the Profintern (the Red International of Labor Unions, or RILU) in the United States. The RILU was a Soviet-created organization to oversee union activities around the world. With War Communism well underway, labor unrest was a valuable way to spread the continued revolution that upended Russia and paved the way for the Bolsheviks to overrun and create the Soviet Union.

Similar to William "Big Bill" Haywood, Foster's labor organizing journey began when he joined the IWW. Foster then continued his organizing on behalf of workers involved in skilled trades and the meat industry (butchers, meat cutters and packinghouse workers), followed by an ambitious plan to direct a wide-scale strike of steelworkers in 1919. Although that period brought about such staples as the eight-hour workday and overtime pay/wage concessions, it was short-lived, as the First World War had ended.

Foster fell out of favor in the 1930s as Browder became leader of the CPUSA. Foster was treated for a heart attack in the Soviet Union in 1932. Only after the Second World War concluded in 1945 was Foster reinstated as a leader of the CPUSA. After his death in 1961, the Soviet Union honored him with a funeral in Red Square. The leader of the procession was Nikita Khrushchev, premier of the Soviet Union, and Foster's ashes are interred partly in the Kremlin Walls, with the other half at Forest Home Cemetery near the Haymarket Affair statue.

Eugene Dennis

After joining the Communist Party in 1926, Eugene Dennis rose through the ranks of the Industrial Workers of the World and as an organizer in California to eventually become general secretary of Communist Party USA. In 1929, Dennis, known then by his birth name, Francis Xavier Waldron, fled to the Soviet Union to avoid prosecution under the California Criminal Syndicalism Act. Syndicalism was a radical strain of the labor movement that promoted strikes and other disruptions throughout industry around the country. He took over as general secretary of the Communist Party (after the falling out of Earl Browder in 1935) when he returned from exile in the Soviet Union.

After the Second World War, in 1948, Dennis and ten other communist leaders were charged with attempting to overthrow the United States government under the Alien Registration Act. Beginning in 1951, Dennis would serve nearly four years in prison before being released in 1955. He continued on as general secretary of the Communist Party and then as party chairman until his death in 1961.

Charles Ruthenberg

The first leader of the Communist Party USA, Charles Ruthenberg worked tirelessly to bring together various factions of socialists under one umbrella. After infighting split the socialists in 1919 at the height of the First Red Scare in the United States, Ruthenberg and fellow communists Louis Fraina and John Reed officially founded Communist Party USA on Blue Island Avenue in Chicago on September 1, 1919. Over the years, Charles Ruthenberg was arrested several times. In 1920, he was arrested on syndicalism charges in Michigan and released after eighteen months at Sing Sing Prison in New York State. In

1925, Ruthenberg was sent to prison again. This time, he was released after a few weeks under an appeal for a retrial. In 1927, he collapsed suddenly and underwent emergency appendectomy surgery, dying three days later.

Thousands packed a memorial meeting at Chicago's Ashland Auditorium—the same hall where Ruthenberg had spoken at the launch of the *Daily Worker* in 1924. In honor of his wishes and at the request of the Communist International, his ashes were conveyed to Moscow, where he was interred just behind Lenin's final resting place.[3]

John Reed, with whom Ruthenberg founded the Communist Party USA in Chicago, was one of the few American eyewitnesses to the Bolshevik revolution in Russia in 1917. Reed documented his experiences in the book *Ten Days that Shook the World*. The 1981 movie *Reds*—starring Warren Beatty, Diane Keaton and Jack Nicholson—was a film adaptation of Reed's book. John Reed died in the Soviet Union in 1920. Reed's remains are located at the Kremlin burial wall, alongside Charles Ruthenberg and other communist sympathizing Americans who are also partially interred at Forest Home Cemetery.

CHICAGO FEDERAL BUILDING BOMBING

On September 4, 1918, someone tossed a bomb into the Adams Street entrance of the Chicago federal building and post office, killing four, including postal workers Edwin Kolkow and William Wheeler, and injuring

Chicago Federal Building explosion, 1918.

dozens of others. The police focused their attention on members of the IWW labor organization. Officers rounded up and arrested almost one hundred members in the early days after the attack; all but a handful were released over the next few days. Despite intense investigations, no convictions ever came from the attack, nor was a reason for the bombing discerned. One of the many postal workers in the building at the time was a substitute letter carrier named Walt Disney.[4]

SEEING RED: THE FIRST RED SCARE OF 1919-20

Most Americans learned and continue to use the catch-all names of Joe McCarthy and McCarthyism as derogatory terms for hunting enemies in their midst and destroying reputations. Few would connect the first Red Scare with the events of Bolshevik Russia taking shape in 1918, as American sympathizers of the Soviet movement were gaining adherents at that time. As troops were returning from the Arctic Circle, an effort to fight the early Bolsheviks, the American Legion was created by veterans of the First World War and chartered in 1919 as a patriotic veteran's service organization by the United States Congress. The Red Menace created an extraordinary sense of anxiety among the public, and these members returning from war were eager to do their part in defending American idealism. Hence, the American Legion included in its charter the promise to "uphold and defend a 100% Americanism" in its preamble. To this day, the same preamble is spoken and referenced at every meeting and convention held by the American Legion in the United States and abroad.

Back on the homefront, a young J. Edgar Hoover was making his mark against the Red Menace as well. Labor unrest was being fomented by communists, anarchists and socialists. Bombs were being sent to various political figures, with deaths and dismemberment common in those violent incidents. As a result, a hard line against radicals and subversives in the United States was undertaken. Various suspects adhering to un-American activities were targeted during the Red Scare in 1919. Raids were authorized by A. Mitchell Palmer, then Justice Department head. The question became what to do with these radicals who were deemed harmful to United States interests. Perhaps if these radicals loved communism so much, why not let them live in Russia? That indeed was what happened, and it was determined that these individuals would become "Christmas presents" for Lenin and Trotsky. In December 1919, a ship commissioned as the USS *Buford* was utilized by the U.S. Navy to send these "presents" to Bolshevik Russia. Using intermediaries, some 249 souls from the United States were sent for a three-month voyage to Finland. (Since there was no diplomatic recognition of the new Bolshevik Russia, the members of the Soviet Ark were dropped off in Finland.) It was at the Finnish border with Russia where these radicals and self-identified communists would walk into the Soviet Union. The Soviets, never shy about pomp and circumstance in these situations, greeted these Christmas presents with cheers and a big band reception playing the Russian national anthem. The 249 members of the Soviet Ark had been hailed as heroes for upholding communist beliefs.

EMMA GOLDMAN

The most famous passenger on the Soviet Ark was Emma Goldman (Lithuanian by birth), who was lecturing in Chicago at the time she was notified of her deportation to Russia in 1919. Goldman had been arrested many times over the years for fomenting labor unrest and promoting socialism and anarchy in the United States. Most notably, Goldman was linked to a violent protest in Chicago called the Haymarket Affair in 1886. In her book *My Disillusionment*, Goldman could barely contain herself while experiencing emotions of finally being in revolutionary Russia: "I could sense the awe and humility of our group who, treated like felons in the United States, were here received as dear brothers and comrades and welcomed by the Red soldiers, the liberators of Russia."

Unfortunately for Emma Goldman, her idealist views of communism—obliterating classes of wealth and championing the working class, thereby entering a new world of idealism—never materialized. She would find herself under house arrest and fled Soviet Russia after nearly a year in that country. After living abroad, she died in Toronto, Canada, in 1940. Emma Goldman is buried alongside these other Soviet and communist sympathizers at the Forest Home Cemetery near Chicago in Forest Park, Illinois.[5]

RISE OF THE WEATHERMEN/WEATHER UNDERGROUND

This organization claimed responsibility for dozens of high-profile bombings, including at police stations, the U.S. Capitol Building and the Pentagon. Oftentimes the bombings were claimed in retaliation for actions by law enforcement, social injustice or protesting policies relating to the Vietnam War. For example, the Pentagon was bombed on Ho Chi Minh's birthday on May 19, 1972. For several years, Bill Ayers and Bernardine Dohrn, along with other Weathermen, were on the run from law enforcement, or "underground." It was not until 1980 that the couple decided to surrender to authorities. It coincided with a splinter of factions in the Weather Underground that saw two camps unfold: those who wanted to surrender and those who remained active or in hiding. The decision to surrender was prompted in part by the birth of two sons to Dohrn and Ayers, as one son was born in 1977 and another in 1980. The couple had married while fugitives from the law.

Context of the Vietnam War

The Vietnam War would become one of the most contentious conflicts in American history. With containment policy proponent George Kennan's foreign policy template guiding America's post–World War II world outlook, communist aggression in Southeast Asia dictated that communist expansion should be met head on by a counteracting force wherever those conflicts should arise. Hence, not sparing an inch or recognition to the North Vietnamese led by Communist Ho Chi Minh, America sent in covert support during the French fall of Dien Bien Phu in 1954. After the French colonial powers withdrew from what would become communist North Vietnam, the United States sent advisers to South Vietnam in its fight against the North. At its height, the Vietnam War would see more than 500,000 American men and women serving in the Vietnam War from 1965 to 1975. The war would spread to, and adversely affect, neighboring countries of Thailand, Laos and Cambodia.

The conflict would be met by protests at home all over the United States. Colleges and universities across the United States were a hotbed of activity, seeing as college-age students were eligible for the military draft. Just north of the Illinois border, at the University of Wisconsin–Madison, the New Year's Gang—Karl Armstrong, Dwight Armstrong, David Fine and Leo

Burt—exploded bombs at Sterling Hall on campus, killing a researcher. The group also defiantly stole a Cessna plane and targeted incendiary devices at the Badger Ammunition Plant in Sauk Prairie on New Year's Eve in 1969, hence the nickname. At a time when the voting age was twenty-one, many students were directly affected by the war since a compulsory draft determined which men would serve during wartime. In 1973, hostilities in the Vietnam War ended with an armistice brokered by Secretary of State Henry Kissinger. The North Vietnamese would dishonor the agreement by invading and overtaking South Vietnam in 1975, actions that culminated in the hostile takeover of Vietnam by the communists. Many Vietnamese, Thai, Laotians and Cambodians would immigrate to the United States, including large numbers to Illinois, after the war ended. More than fifty-six thousand combat or combat-related casualties of American men and women are listed on the Vietnam War Memorial in Washington, D.C.

You Don't Need a Weatherman to Know Which Way the Wind Blows

The New Left of the 1960s was a movement of like-minded groups formed in the era of civil rights, social justice/inequality and opposition to the Vietnam War. These groups were composed of mostly white, college-aged students. Students for a Democratic Society (SDS) was the most notable of the era, although there were numerous organizations dedicated to the cause. In 1969, Bernardine Dohrn authored a manifesto titled *You Don't Need a Weatherman to Know Which Way the Wind Blows*. The manifesto rather bluntly stated that "the goal [of revolution] is the destruction of U.S. imperialism and the achievement of a classless world: world communism." During an annual SDS meeting in Chicago that year, the SDS collapsed and the Revolutionary Youth Movement, led by Ayers and Dohrn, would succeed in its stead. Thereafter, this group became known as the Weathermen. By October 1970, Bernardine Dohrn, a former high school cheerleader and National Honor Society member from a tony suburb of Milwaukee, had been placed on the FBI's Ten Most Wanted Fugitives list.

Declaration of a State of War

Direct confrontation would devolve into strategic action. Dohrn was a principal signatory on the Weather Underground's "Declaration of a State of War" in May 1970 that formally declared "war" on the U.S. government. This completed the group's transformation from political advocacy to violent action. She went so far as to record the declaration and sent a transcript of a tape recording to the *New York Times*. Dohrn and Bill Ayers collaborated on another revolutionary manifesto titled "Prairie Fire" in 1974, furthering the group's literature in its quest.

Later, in December 1969, the group held a "War Council" in Flint, Michigan, where plans were finalized to change into an underground organization that would commit strategic acts of sabotage against the government at all levels. Thereafter, it was called Weather Underground Organization (WUO).

Haymarket Affair and Ties to the Days of Rage

In an homage to the 1886 labor demonstration in Haymarket, Chicago, the Days of Rage maintained a symbiotic relationship to demonstrators past who had spoken out and brought attention to inequality in the late nineteenth century. As mentioned earlier in this chapter, in the midst of the protest, an unidentified person threw a bomb into the crowd as speakers promoted labor and justice reforms. This action resulted in a deadly riot in which both protesters and police died. The entire episode was blamed on anarchists.

Nearly a century later, on October 6, 1969, shortly before the Days of Rage riots organized by the Weathermen, protesters blew up a statue in Chicago commemorating the police casualties from the Haymarket Riot. The statue was rebuilt; exactly one year later, the Weathermen blew it up again. Once again the statue was rebuilt, and a twenty-four-hour police guard kept watch over it. Despite the presence of security, the Weathermen blew it up once more. It was rebuilt a fourth instance, this time at the Chicago police headquarters, where it has remained largely intact ever since.

CHAPTER 2

RONALD REAGAN

VICTORY OVER COMMUNISM

"TEAR DOWN THIS WALL!"

Behind me stands a wall that encircles the free sectors of this city, part of a vast system of barriers that divides the entire continent of Europe… Standing before the Brandenburg Gate, every man is a German, separated from his fellow men. Every man is a Berliner, forced to look upon a scar… As long as this gate is closed, as long as this scar of a wall is permitted to stand, it is not the German question alone that remains open, but the question of freedom for all mankind.…

General Secretary Gorbachev, if you seek peace, if you seek prosperity for the Soviet Union and Eastern Europe, if you seek liberalization, come here to this gate.

Mr. Gorbachev, open this gate!

Mr. Gorbachev, tear down this wall![6]

These words, evoked in a speech at the Brandenburg Gate in West Berlin by Ronald Reagan on June 12, 1987, were a punctuation mark not simply on his presidency but on a vision to take on the Soviet Union directly to rid the world of communism. For decades, Reagan had lambasted detente, the United States' foreign policy designed to thaw the Cold War and espoused by Richard Nixon, Gerald Ford and Jimmy Carter. That approach had allowed the Soviet Union and its client states in Eastern Europe to maintain the status quo, imprisoning millions to a hopeless and destitute fate.

Prophetic as it may have been, the Berlin Wall would come crashing down nearly two years later, on November 9, 1989. The world watched with awe as the largest symbol dividing East and West was to be no more. East and West Berliners passed through an otherwise heavily guarded and fortified military border, similar to the Demilitarized Zone dividing North and South Korea. For the first time in decades, Berliners could freely move between East and West. Families, friends, relatives and complete strangers shared joy and bonds that had been impossible for generations.

Although the Berlin Wall falling occurred less than a year after his leaving office, the magnificent event was attributed to Reagan's position toward the Soviet Union during his tenure. Reagan would play host to many events, infamous or otherwise, that would endear the public to him as well. The United States until that time saw the largest peacetime economic expansion in American history, as well as a disruption of the malaise that America went through during the 1970s and, in particular, the Jimmy Carter administration, which preceded Reagan's administration. In contrast to the gas lines of that decade, oil prices dropped precipitously in 1986, affecting the United States manufacturing system. The Soviets, ever reliant on exporting oil for the lifeblood of their economy, suffered tremendously as a result.

"HE MIGHT GROW UP TO BE PRESIDENT SOMEDAY"

Ronald Wilson Reagan was born to Nelle and Jack Reagan in Tampico, Illinois, on February 6, 1911. When his father, Jack, first looked at his newborn son, a ten-pound baby, he said, "He looks like a fat little Dutchman. But who knows, he might grow up to be president someday."[7] Ronald Reagan would live the first three years of his life in the apartment building in which he was born, above a tavern, until moving into another house in Tampico shortly thereafter. His family then moved around various cities in Illinois, including Monmouth, Galesburg and even Chicago, before settling into what is considered his boyhood home in Dixon, Illinois. Moving around many cities was due to the economic conditions and Jack's inability to hold a job for long periods of time. It was said that Jack's drinking caused many firings and layoffs, but Reagan father eventually settled into a job at a local shoe store in Dixon.

Ronald Reagan as a boy in Dixon, Illinois.

THE REAGAN BOYS LIVED A TYPICAL LIFE

As a young boy growing up in Dixon, Reagan often recalled his youthful shenanigans, including one incident where he was lighting and throwing "torpedoes" (firecrackers) across a bridge in town that sparked a colorful commotion. Recently, the town had banned fireworks within the city limits. After he lit the fireworks, an unmarked car drove alongside the young boy. A man wearing a suit and a fedora, akin to Eliot Ness, was driving the vehicle. The man motioned Reagan to get in the car. Reagan responded by using a nursery rhyme in a clever way:

> *Twinkle, twinkle little star*
> *Who the hell do you think you are?*

Unbeknownst to young Ronald, the man driving the car was the chief of police. Reagan was subsequently arrested for the fireworks violation, and the chief likely didn't think his retort was humorous at all. Jack was called and had to pay a nearly fifteen-dollar fine. By comparison, in those times fifteen dollars was equal to a month's rent.

In a more subtle dig at authority, a youthful Reagan would often find or save pennies by working odd jobs. Since he and his brother, Neil, shared a bedroom, Ronald would have to take measures to hide his earnings so Neil did not steal them for his own use. Ronald found the perfect spot: loose tiles that were adjacent to the fireplace in the sitting room of the Reagan residence. The tiles could be easily slid back and forth, as well as pulled up and down, whereby only the keenest observer could recognize any displacement of length, width or depth the size of a penny.[8]

But another obstacle presented itself: young Ronald was not allowed to set foot inside the sitting room other than special occasions for family functions and permission granted by his mother. Rest assured, a way around this rule was found and bent to Ronald's advantage. Since he was a lanky boy, Ronald did his bidding by placing his feet at the entrance to the sitting room. From there, he would stretch across the floor, move the tiles to his liking and place the pennies underneath for safe keeping. In the event his mother would charge him for disobeying her rule, Reagan could claim he didn't set a foot in the room at all.

Ronald Reagan, First Lady Nancy and Neil Reagan visited the boyhood home in Dixon in February 1984. After seeing how it was refurbished by the caretakers, Ronald Reagan quipped that he would have liked living in the newer version. He insisted on dining at the table later that cold winter day, and the Secret Service went through great pains to ensure the safety of the president, Nancy and Neil. After all, even a simple meal is considered a complex undertaking in these circumstances.

All was not mischief with Ronald and Neil. They were avid readers and spent many days reading at the Dixon Public Library. Ronald worked odd jobs throughout his childhood and found his calling as a lifeguard for many years along the Rock River. He is credited with saving seventy-seven lives. It has been said that many of those "saved" were young women seeking the adoration of the affable and handsome lifeguard. After graduating from high school, Reagan attended nearby Eureka College, where he majored in economics.

After college, Reagan became a radio announcer for multiple stations in Iowa, announcing games for the Chicago Cubs. He and the station relied on wire transmissions to give basic play-by-play descriptions of what was happening far away. On more than one occasion, Reagan recalled, the transmission was delayed for a few minutes at a time. Instead of dead air, which was a cardinal sin in the radio business, Reagan simply made up a fictional account of the game. Upon the return of transmission service, he was relieved that the game was playing as scheduled and picked up where the baseball game had left off, the audience unaware of the disruption.[9]

In 1937, Reagan made his big break into show business. While in Los Angeles for a Cubs game, he passed a screen test for Warner Bros. and signed a seven-year contract. Relegated to the "B" film unit, he would go on to appear in the football film *Knute Rockne, All American*. Reagan would appear in films with such actors as Humphrey Bogart, Bette Davis and Errol Flynn. He also appeared with future wife Nancy Davis in the movie *Hellcats of the Navy*.

After his service in the army during the Second World War, Reagan returned to Hollywood and was elected president of the Screen Actors Guild in 1947. He was elected six times to the post and served the guild through 1961. A noted anti-communist, Reagan would steer the guild through the Hollywood Blacklist era. At one point, Reagan became an FBI informant, and after his first child, Maureen, was born, the Reagans feared for their lives. Reagan armed himself and the household with a gun.

In the 1950s, Reagan moved into television, notably with General Electric Theater, where he became a national household name. In 1964, he made a terrific speech on behalf of Barry Goldwater, "A Time to Choose." During his speech, Reagan spelled out the principles of freedom he stood for, the limited role of government:

> *Not too long ago, two friends of mine were talking to a Cuban refugee, a businessman who had escaped from [Fidel] Castro, and in the midst of his story one of my friends turned to the other and said, "We don't know how lucky we are." And the Cuban stopped and said, "How lucky you are? I had someplace to escape to." And in that sentence he told us the entire story. If we lose freedom here, there's no place to escape to. This is the last stand on earth.*
>
> *And this idea that government is beholden to the people, that it has no other source of power except the sovereign people, is still the newest and the most unique idea in all the long history of man's relation to man.*
>
> *This is the issue of this election: Whether we believe in our capacity for self-government or whether we abandon the American revolution and confess that a little intellectual elite in a far-distant capitol can plan our lives for us better than we can plan them ourselves.*
>
> *You and I are told increasingly we have to choose between a left or right. Well I'd like to suggest there is no such thing as a left or right. There's only an up or down—up to man's age-old dream, the ultimate in individual freedom consistent with law and order, or down to the ant heap of totalitarianism. And regardless of their sincerity, their humanitarian motives, those who would trade our freedom for security have embarked on this downward course.*[10]

GOVERNOR OF CALIFORNIA

Fresh off his rousing speech for Barry Goldwater, the Republican Party of California nominated Ronald Reagan as its gubernatorial candidate in the 1966 election. An inexperienced politician, Reagan used his genuineness and his ability to connect with the people in his quest for office. When asked by a reporter how he would perform in office, Reagan replied, "I don't know. I've never played a governor." Reagan would go on to defeat the two-term Democrat Pat Brown with 57 percent of the vote, over 1 million votes. His biggest challenges of the era involved the antiwar protesters at the University of California–Berkeley, welfare reform and a balanced budget for the State of California. In 1976, after his second term expired as governor, Reagan

Actor Chuck Connors stumping for Ronald Reagan during his run for governor.

California governor Ronald Reagan with son Ron, wife Nancy and daughter Patti.

challenged for the Republican nomination, only to fall 60 votes short. He would then wait another four years before running and ultimately winning the presidency in 1980.

REAGAN AND THE CREW OF THE USS *PUEBLO*, 1968

The year 1968 was a watershed one for disruption in the United States and around the world. The Tet Offensive was launched by the North Vietnamese in late January. The offensive was a military victory by the United States forces but a PR disaster back home. Martin Luther King Jr. was assassinated in April, and Bobby Kennedy would follow in June while running for the Democratic Party nomination. The Democratic Convention itself was in turmoil in Chicago, witnessing angry riots and fights on the convention floor. Riots and marches protesting the Vietnam War were consuming

Washington, D.C., and cities around the United States. Later that summer, in Czechoslovakia, the Prague Spring would be crushed by Soviet forces.

The USS *Pueblo* and its crew had been held hostage inside North Korea for eleven months before the crew was released back to the United States. As governor of California in 1968, Ronald Reagan greeted the crew upon its return. He was one of the few outspoken critics of the Johnson and Kennedy administrations on foreign policy, and the *Pueblo* incident in 1968 was no exception. Reagan was asked about the *Pueblo* in many campaign speeches that year. He went so far as to create a campaign film called "Ronald Reagan, Citizen Governor," whereby Reagan launched scathing attacks on foreign policy and military failures of the Kennedy-Johnson years. Reagan made the *Pueblo* a cornerstone of his criticisms of America's recent foreign affairs debacles. "The seizure of the *Pueblo* and the kidnapping of our men is a humiliation we will not endure." he stated.[11]

Richard Rogala of Oak Brook, Illinois, was one of eighty-two prisoners from the *Pueblo* held in captivity in North Korea for eleven months. During his imprisonment, he and the crew were given the equivalent of slop to eat, served in buckets with a stench alongside the flies and maggots. The food was no different than what the animals were fed. The crew lost weight on an unbelievable scale, to the point that many of the crew members were gaunt due to undernourishment, stress and mistreatment. The crew was under constant harassment and forced to confess and admit to being spies of the United States. Captain Pete Buchar, in particular, took a lot of heat for his men, losing more than one-third of his weight; he was beaten mercilessly and forced to sign a "confession" admitting his violation of North Korean sovereignty.

Rogala shared his version of "Hell Week," in which the crew members were beaten severely for giving a "Hawaiian Good Luck" sign regularly to their North Korean captors. The sign, of course, was the middle finger, often given in passing as the crew in captivity was passing down the corridors past the guards. *TIME* magazine, in its quest to showcase the resistance that the eighty-two prisoners demonstrated during their classroom sessions learning socialism, printed a front-page photo of the men demonstrating the "Hawaiian Good Luck" sign on October 18, 1968. When the North Koreans learned what the sign actually meant, "Hell Week" ensued. Rogala vividly remembered being ordered to kneel down in front of the guards and then barked at to "Stand up!" whereby he would be punched or hit with the butt of a rifle. This was repeated continuously and barbarically until Rogala had very few remaining healthy teeth.[12]

Governor Reagan greeting the crew of the USS *Pueblo* upon return, 1968.

The USS *Pueblo* remains inside North Korea in Pyongyang as of this writing, held at the Victorious Fatherland Liberation War Museum. To their credit, the North Koreans painted the ship and took efforts to refurbish their "trophy" to serve as a reminder of their prestige on the world stage. The ship is the only registered and commissioned U.S. naval vessel held in foreign hands as of this writing. A guide during a tour by the author of the USS *Pueblo* in 2015 gave an unapologetic handling of the captive prisoners. She stated that the crew was well fed and given warm clothes and plenty of exercise. In reality, the crew members were underfed, allowed only a few minutes in the exercise yard and were freezing. They were routinely beaten in order to extract "confessions." The tour guide also claimed that the American government was not interested in having the crew back. She cited the eleven months they were held as prisoners of war and how the United States would not capitulate and sign a letter of apology and conspiracy against the DPRK. In the end, the crew was released on December 23, 1968.

1980

Ronald Reagan ran for president as a political outsider in 1980, hailing from California but exhibiting his midwestern roots in Illinois. The American people enthusiastically embraced the former Hollywood actor and governor of California in defeat of Jimmy Carter in 1980. Ever the establishment wrecking ball, Reagan went against the grain by firmly believing in the American people. Jimmy Carter's America was weakened by such high inflation and astronomical interest rates that a "misery index" was created. Long gas lines and the Iranian hostage crisis also befell Carter, who otherwise was looked on as a decent man. However, a decent man did not make an extraordinary leader, as the Iranian hostage situation turned worse when the United States military made a deadly and failed incursion into Iran to free the remaining fifty-two American hostages with an elite force. Instead, the operation was aborted when a sandstorm delayed the mission. A helicopter also crashed into a transport plane, and in total eight American servicemen died in the boondoggle, reflecting poorly on Carter. Ronald Reagan would win the election in a landslide with more than 50 percent of the popular vote and an enormous Electoral College victory of 489–44, carrying forty-four states in the process. Reagan was the oldest person elected president of the United States at the age of sixty-nine.

Reagan would be reelected in a landslide in 1984 against the Democratic ticket of Walter Mondale and Geraldine Ferraro. So unequivocally humorous was Reagan that, when asked about being the oldest elected president in a debate, he signaled to Mondale by stating, "I will not make age an issue of this campaign. I am not going to exploit, for political purposes, my opponent's youth and inexperience."

Ronald Reagan would not just be known for his role in defining the evils of communism and the fall of the Soviet Union during his tenure as president of the United States. He also survived an unsuccessful assassination attempt in 1981, ushered in the use of the NASA space shuttle, helped heal the nation during the *Challenger* space shuttle explosion, responded to the Chernobyl disaster and grappled with the Iran-Contra affair during his second term in office. Reagan would also figure into the fight over the politicization of Supreme Court nominees with his nomination of Justice Robert Bork in 1987, a University of Chicago law school graduate. U.S. Supreme Court nominations would change dramatically into partisan affairs, despite most appointments prior to the Bork nomination often drawing little scrutiny and often receiving overwhelming support in the Senate chamber.

Assassination Attempt in 1981

Much is stated about where people were and what they experienced during seminal events. The events of September 11 are a contemporary example for those who lived during the attacks on the World Trade Center towers, in Pennsylvania and at the Pentagon by Islamic militant terrorists in 2001. The Kennedy era left a remarkable impression on those coming of age in that generation. The Bay of Pigs invasion of Cuba, the Cuban Missile Crisis and the culmination of his assassination left an indelible mark on their lives. Usually, they were school memories, as my parents and colleagues grew up in the 1960s. My memories are no different.

My third-grade class was having a routine day on March 30, 1981, at Madison Elementary School in Janesville, but the afternoon turned into a national emergency. Our teacher received a phone call over the intercom and quickly turned on the television in the classroom. Televisions were a rarity in classrooms unless it was wheeled in on a cart for a particular current events program or children's news segment for that morning. The initial reaction was for her to purposely block the screen in case images of blood or death were seen. A scuffle ensued outside the Washington Hilton Hotel, where the president had been giving a speech. He was confronted by John Hinckley Jr., who managed to fire shots at Reagan and others, hitting the president, police officer Thomas Delahanty and Secret Service agent Tim McCarthy, as well as Reagan's assistant James Brady. The Secret Service bodyguard shoved Reagan into his vehicle, bumping Reagan's head in the process. Reagan survived the shooting, having undergone surgery to remove the bullet. Nancy Reagan rushed to the hospital and found her husband losing considerable blood; an oxygen mask was assisting his breathing. The president famously said, "Honey, I forgot to duck." Ever a sharp wit, Reagan would have one last message before undergoing a procedure to remove the bullet. Before going under sedation, the president stated to surgeons, "I hope you're all Republicans."

In a further sign of his indelible sense of humor and timing, Reagan was giving a speech in West Berlin but two months later. A balloon popped unexpectedly at the celebratory speech. Without missing a beat from his speech, Reagan paused momentarily and quipped, "Missed me."

Chernobyl Nuclear Reactor Explosion April 1986

Chernobyl has caught the imagination of many after more than thirty years, as that fateful day on April 26, 1986, became the worst nuclear disaster in the Soviet-dominated Ukraine. Four reactors were online when the Chernobyl incident took place. A fifth reactor was nearly 80 percent complete when disaster struck. Reactor no. 4 was the subject of a test on the evening of April 26, 1986, when steam contributed to an explosion of epic proportions. The Soviets did not report anything officially immediately on the accident. Without direct acknowledgement from the normally secretive Soviets, speculation was that a dangerous and adverse nuclear event had occurred, based on instrumentation readings in Western Europe. The instruments were detecting ever-larger radiation readings taking place and moving closer to the Atlantic Ocean. In many ways Chernobyl would spell the beginning of the end of the Soviet Union. Many of its military helicopters and helicopter pilots were recalled from Afghanistan to douse the fire with chemicals and concrete from the air, further complicating Soviet occupation of that country.

The town of Chernobyl itself is about ten miles south of the reactor sites. However, being the principal town near the Chernobyl nuclear plants, its name was assigned to the reactor sites established in 1970. Chernobyl is a beautiful natural area akin to Illinois and Wisconsin. Plush vegetation, trees, foliage and the blue water of the Pripyat River would fool any person unaware of the history of the area. If it were functioning without its ominous and dangerous past, the area would be utilized as a resort destination for camping, hiking, water sports and fishing. Instead, it would be Chernobyl's fate to be remembered as the world's worst nuclear disaster site.

Remarkably, only one person died as a direct cause of the explosion. The other immediate deaths would harshly befall emergency response personnel and firefighters, called "liquidators." Dozens perished as they doused the flames, provided medical care and assessed the situation. All of those responding to the eruption perished, with scant understanding exactly what they were fighting. Today, visitors can come within about two hundred feet of reactor no. 4, just outside the fence line guarding the reactor. The original sarcophagus placed on the reactor after the explosion was replaced a few short months after the visit, several years overdue and over budget.

Reagan's Reaction to Chernobyl

Ronald Reagan was very terse in response to the Chernobyl disaster. On April 30, Reagan wrote in his diary, "This was to be a day off....It was interrupted by a briefing on the nuclear plan emergency in Chernobyl Russia. As usual the Russians won't put out any facts but it is evident that a radioactive cloud is spreading beyond the Soviet border."[13]

"A nuclear accident that results in contaminating a number of countries with radioactive material is not simply an internal matter," Reagan declared in his regular Saturday radio address, which was taped in Tokyo, where he and the leaders of six other major industrialized democracies were opening their twelfth economic summit meeting. "The Soviets owe the world an explanation," the president said. "A full accounting of what happened at Chernobyl and what is happening now is the least the world community has a right to expect."[14]

Soviet leader Mikhail Gorbachev, on cue, finally responded to the tragedy in a public address. In doing so, he also accused the United States of launching an "unrestrained anti-Soviet campaign" based on a "mountain of lies" meant to discredit the Soviets. In another response to the Chernobyl incident, President Reagan offered humanitarian assistance to the Soviets. The Soviet Union rebuffed the offer, despite medical assistance being needed in such a disaster. In response, the Medical College of Wisconsin in Milwaukee sprang into action. Dr. Mortimer Bortin had maintained an International Bone Marrow Transplant Registry at the medical college. He and a team of doctors assisted patients inside the Soviet Union and saved many lives as a result.

Challenger *Space Shuttle Explosion in January 1986*

The *Challenger* explosion is a tragedy in its own right, with the loss of several astronauts. What made this particular mission even worse was that it was to carry the first teacher into space, Christa MacCauliffe. A teacher from New Hampshire, MacCauliffe was selected out of an applicant pool of ten thousand teachers. The idea was to have not only a civilian in space but also the first teacher, who would lead lessons for schoolchildren while in orbit on the space shuttle *Challenger*.

As alluded to earlier, every generation has vivid moments of "where they were" when seminal events occur. The *Challenger* explosion is another of those frightening, tragic events that are very well remembered. While we were sitting in class in eighth grade, a sullen announcement over the intercom noted that disaster had struck early that morning in January. Televisions showed the launch over and over, beginning with the shuttle blasting off the launch pad without incident. Less than a minute later, the explosion caused the shuttle clouds to drift left and right. Spectators on the ground at Cape Canaveral were stunned. Well into the evening, our eyes would be glued to the television sets, hoping against all odds that the astronauts could have a sliver of a chance of making it out alive. In Congressional hearings and commission findings, it was discovered that the O-rings on the boosters were faulty.

Iran-Contra Affair and the Negotiated Hostage Releases in the Middle East

The Iran-Contra affair was a seminal moment in Cold War history in the 1980s. The Sandinista government in Nicaragua took charge after deposing the dictator Antonio Somoza in 1979. In his anti-communist crusade, Ronald Reagan backed the Contras in Nicaragua, who were fighting against the pro-Marxist/pro-Soviet Sandinista government. When Democrats in Congress blocked the funding of these "freedom fighters," the Reagan administration sought other ways to support the Contras. A plan was hatched to sell arms (notably tube-fired anti-tank and antiaircraft missiles) to Iran in exchange for its help securing the release of American hostages in the Middle East. At that time, Iran was embroiled in a war with its neighbor, Iraq, led by Saddam Hussein. The proceeds of these arms sales were then funneled to assist the Contras in Nicaragua.

Eugene Hasenfus, a former United States Marine from Marinette, Wisconsin, would be at the center of the incident. A cargo plane carrying weapons intended for the Contras was shot down by the Sandinistas on October 5, 1986. Hasenfus was the only survivor. He was tried and convicted in Nicaragua, and on November 15, 1986, he was sentenced to thirty years in prison for terrorism and other charges. He was released in December of that year.[15]

Hearings on Capitol Hill were held in prime time, with cameras awaiting Colonel Oliver North, who had arranged the monies between intermediaries in the Iranian government who presented themselves as moderates. Colonel North was a point man in trading anti-tank weapons and AWAC (early air warning systems) equipment to the Iranian government in its fight against Iraq during the Iran-Iraq War from 1980 to 1988. While the United States was no friend of the Iranians, there certainly was no love lost for Iraq dictator Saddam Hussein either. The Soviets, as usual, were lurking and meddling in influence in the Middle East as well. The purpose was to arrange for American hostages to be freed in Lebanon, and several of the long-held hostages, like Terry Anderson, were freed as a result of the underhanded dealings that occurred. On the final days of George H.W. Bush's tenure as president in January 1993, he pardoned several of the Iran-Contra figures.

RONALD REAGAN'S LEGACY

Ronald Reagan brought an optimism long lost to the United States, which had experienced malaise and economic hardships during the 1970s. His critics point out that his tax cutting and increased military spending created budget deficits throughout his tenure as president. The economy grew by leaps and bounds, however, and created the longest peacetime expansion in

Gorbachev, Reagan and George Bush in New York City, 1988.

American history up to that point. He also helped set in motion the end of the Soviet Union and negotiated actual reductions in nuclear armaments with the Soviet Union, de-escalating the Arms Race in the process.

Reagan left office one of the most popular presidents in recent memory and is still regarded as a standard-bearer of conservatism and one of the most personable politicians ever. Reagan had planned an active post-presidency career after his second term expired. However, news of Alzheimer's disease was taking its toll. It was announced formally in 1994 that the former president was suffering from the debilitating disease. He passed away in 2003 and is buried at the Ronald Reagan Presidential Library in Simi Valley, California.

CHAPTER 3

ERNEST HEMINGWAY

A COLD WAR JOURNEY

Ernest Miller Hemingway was born at eight o'clock in the morning on July 21, 1899, in Oak Park, Illinois. In the nearly sixty-two years of his life that followed, he forged a literary reputation unsurpassed in the twentieth century. In doing so, he also created a mythological hero in himself that captivated (and at times confounded) not only serious literary critics but the average man as well. In a word, he was a star.

Born in the family home at 439 North Oak Park Avenue (now 339 North Oak Park Avenue), a house built by his widowed grandfather, Ernest Hall, Hemingway was the second of Dr. Clarence and Grace Hall Hemingway's six children; he had four sisters and one brother. He was named after his maternal grandfather, Ernest Hall, and his great-uncle, Miller Hall.

Oak Park was a mainly Protestant, upper middle-class suburb of Chicago that Hemingway would later refer to as a town of "wide lawns and narrow minds." Only ten miles from the big city, Oak Park was really much further away philosophically. It was basically a conservative town that tried to isolate itself from Chicago's liberal seediness. Hemingway was raised with the conservative midwestern values of strong religion, hard work, physical fitness and self-determination; if one adhered to these parameters, he was taught, success in whatever field he chose would be ensured.

As a boy, he was taught by his father to hunt and fish along the shores and in the forests surrounding Lake Michigan. The Hemingway's had a summer house called Windemere on Walloon Lake in northern Michigan, and the family would spend the summer months there trying to stay cool.

Ernest Hemingway at home in Oak Park.

Hemingway would either fish the different streams that ran into the lake or would take the rowboat out to do some fishing there. He would also go squirrel hunting in the woods near the summer house, discovering early in life the serenity to be found while alone in the forest or wading a stream. It was something he could always go back to throughout his life, wherever he was. Nature would be the touchstone of Hemingway's life and work, and although he often found himself living in major cities like Chicago, Toronto and Paris early in his career, once he became successful, he chose somewhat isolated places to live like Key West or San Francisco de Paula, Cuba, or Ketchum, Idaho. All were convenient locales for hunting and fishing.

When he wasn't hunting or fishing, his mother taught him the finer points of music. Grace was an accomplished singer who once had aspirations of a career on stage, but she eventually settled down with her husband and occupied her time by giving voice and music lessons to local children, including her own. Hemingway never had a knack for music and suffered through choir practices and cello lessons; however, the musical knowledge he acquired from his mother helped him share in his first wife Hadley's interest in the piano.

Hemingway received his formal schooling in the Oak Park public school system. In high school, he was mediocre at sports, playing football, swimming, water basketball and serving as the track team manager. He enjoyed working on the high school newspaper called the *Trapeze*, where he wrote his first articles, usually humorous pieces in the style of Ring Lardner, a popular satirist of the time. Hemingway graduated in the spring of 1917, and instead of going to college the following fall like his parents expected, he took a job as a cub reporter for the *Kansas City Star*; the job was arranged for by his Uncle Tyler, who was a close friend of the chief editorial writer of the paper.

FIRST WORLD WAR: ITALIAN AMBULANCE DRIVER

Hemingway first visited Italy in 1918 as a young man off to battle. As World War I raged in the north, an eighteen-year-old Hemingway volunteered to drive an ambulance for the Red Cross on the Italian front. In addition to delivering wounded soldiers to safety, he transported supplies.

On one such mission—delivering cigarettes and chocolate—a mortar shell exploded only steps away from where he stood, leaving him with more than two hundred shrapnel wounds. Despite his injuries, the young man dragged an Italian soldier to safety. For his courage, Hemingway was awarded the Italian Silver Medal of Bravery. He spent the next six months recovering in an army hospital in Milano, where he fell in love with a nurse who eventually left him for an Italian soldier. She was the first woman to break his heart.

Ernest Hemingway in World War I uniform.

These early experiences of life, death and love shaped the young writer. Ten years later, he recounted the period in *A Farewell to Arms*, the novel about a wounded soldier and his nurse that cemented Hemingway's stature as a modern American writer.

HEMINGWAY IN SPAIN

For Ernest Hemingway, the fight against General Francisco Franco became a cause of utmost importance. In March 1937, he traveled to Madrid to observe conditions firsthand. Reporting on the war for the North American Newspaper Alliance (NANA), Hemingway penned thirty-one dispatches from Spain. He also helped produce a pro-Republican film, *The Spanish Earth*. His experiences during that civil war provided the material for what many consider to be Hemingway's most famous novel, *For Whom the Bell Tolls* (1940). The film version touches on debates related to Hemingway's presence in Spain and his actions on behalf of the republic.

During his earlier years living in Paris, Hemingway spent a great deal of time in Pamplona watching bullfights and learning about the contests. He became an aficionado of the sport and followed the matches closely. After leaving Paris, Hemingway returned in the early 1930s to do research for his manifesto on the subject, *Death in the Afternoon*. Hemingway visited Spain often and attended bullfights throughout his life. His last trip to the country in 1959 to watch the contests between two famous matadors lead to the *LIFE* magazine story "The Dangerous Summer."

Hemingway's time in Cuba began in 1928, when he visited the island, setting up residence there for both leisurely and writing pursuits. Cuba had been dominated by the United States influence since the Spanish-American War of 1898. The island went through dictators and strongmen. Carlos

Children in Spain during the Spanish Civil War.

Prío Socarrás had taken over the island nation in a putsch. Soon he would be overthrown in favor of Fulgencio Batista. Batista was a military general who lavished himself and his ardent supporters to gain favor ruling over the island. In the 1950s, Che Guevara and Fidel Castro would succeed in overthrowing the United States–backed Batista, who had seen that U.S. agricultural, business and casino interests were favorable toward its larger northern neighbor.[16]

Spanish Civil War: Abraham Lincoln Brigade in Spain

In 1936, a large contingent of American "fellow travelers" to the communist cause went to Spain to fight on behalf of the republic. Francisco Franco was supported by Nazi Germany, and the country of Spain was engulfed in an endless civil war. During its run through 1939, almost 40,000 men and women from fifty-two countries, including 2,800 Americans, volunteered to travel to Spain and join the International Brigades to help fight fascism. The U.S. volunteers served in various units and came to be known collectively as the Abraham Lincoln Brigade.[17]

CUBA

In 1940, Hemingway, with his new wife, Martha, purchased a home outside Havana, Cuba. He would live there for the next twenty years. The Hemingway's named the site Finca Vigia, or "Lookout Farm." They shared their home with dozens of Hemingway's beloved cats, as well as trophies from many successful hunts and fishing expeditions.

Hemingway became a fixture of Havana and stayed in the country longer than many Americans had chosen to after relations between Cuba and the United States began to deteriorate. He fished extensively aboard his boat, *Pilar*, and enjoyed the island lifestyle, hanging out in Havana and entertaining guests at the Finca. His home—with many original furnishings, hunting trophies and personal artifacts—can be viewed today.

When not fishing or traveling, Hemingway wrote a great deal from his Cuban home. While little of his work from this time was published during his lifetime, many of the projects that Hemingway worked on throughout the 1940s were later edited and published after his death.

Hemingway the World War II journalist.

Hemingway continued his war reporting during his time in Cuba. He and Martha traveled to China in 1941 to report on the Second Sino-Japanese War for *PM* magazine. After returning from China, and before heading to Europe to cover World War II, Hemingway hunted German U-boats in the Caribbean from *Pilar*, which he had outfitted with radio communications and weaponry should his craft encounter a German submarine.

In 1944, Hemingway traveled to Europe to report on World War II. His first stop was in London, where he wrote about the war's effect on the city. It was in London that he met a fellow reporter, Mary Welsh, who would later become his fourth wife. They traveled together in England and then on to the French coast and Paris, following the Allied forces as they first invaded Normandy and eventually liberated the French capital. Hemingway spent some time in Paris and later traveled with American forces as they entered Germany before returning home. Hemingway divorced Martha in 1945 and returned to Cuba in 1946. He married Mary Welsh, and she joined him at the Finca.

Hemingway worked for some time on what would become his most famous work, *The Old Man and the Sea*. Originally published in 1952 in its entirety in a single issue of *LIFE* magazine, sales exceeded all expectations. In addition to wide acclaim and financial success, *The Old Man and the Sea* also garnered Hemingway a Pulitzer Prize in 1953, as well as the Nobel Prize in Literature in 1954.

After Fidel Castro took power in 1959, Hemingway continued his stay in Cuba. Long familiar and close with many Cuban people, Hemingway went out of his way to invite Castro and Che Guevara deep sea fishing. Castro, by his own luck and fortune, caught two marlins in an otherwise difficult sport his first time casting lines. By 1961, depression had already set in on the famed author. Hemingway turned down an opportunity to attend John F. Kennedy's inauguration. He would take his life in Idaho later that year in July. Hemingway's home in Havana continues to be a tourist attraction for the Cuban government.

CHAPTER 4

ESPIONAGE

A WEAPON OF THE COLD WAR

In 1949, Americans and western countries cringed as the Soviet Union tested its first nuclear bomb. No longer did the United States have a monopoly on this super weapon that had caused the Japanese empire to surrender to the Allies in 1945, ending the Second World War. The year 1949 also bore witness to communist Mao Zedong and his forces marching into Peking (now Beijing) and driving the Nationalist forces off the continent to the island of Formosa (now Taiwan). A Soviet agent embedded in the Manhattan Project during the Second World War would be partially responsible for the USSR gaining usage of an atomic bomb. In early 1950, Klaus Fuchs would confess to being a Soviet spy. He stayed on in other atomic science capacity projects until 1949, when he was unmasked.

The second Red Scare was also well underway in 1948, as the House Un-American Activities Committee was ferreting out communists and fellow travelers deeply entrenched in the government. Richard Nixon, then congressman from California, was awash in testimony from such figures as Alger Hiss and Whittaker Chambers linking Hiss's influence as a Soviet collaborator to the fall of China. In a precursor to McCarthy's own allegations and investigations, those accused of communism or communist sympathies would be surrounded by friends and professional acquaintances vouching for their innocence and condemning hearings and accusations, including many who worked at the higher levels of government. Allegations would prove correct in many cases when the Venona Decrypts were finally declassified in 1995. Venona proved that Hiss, like many others, such as

Harry Dexter White and Harry Hopkins and other New Deal progressives, had indeed some connection to the KGB or Soviet espionage.

One of the principal features of war, under any circumstances, is information and the need to know what the "other side" is doing. Of course, the world of espionage is nothing new, and the price for being caught is as much a reality as those reaping the rewards of a dangerous game. General George Washington turned to Nathan Hale to spy during the American Revolutionary War against the British. Hale would pay the ultimate price for his actions. During the American Civil War, stories abound whereby women would infiltrate both Union and Confederate sides of the conflict as caretakers and cooks. Women would famously hide papers, swords, pistols and other war materiel in their hoop skirts. Mata Hari, the famous singer and dancer, was convicted of being a German spy during the First World War and executed by a French firing squad in 1917.

The age of the Cold War brought about unique methods in addition to old-fashioned information networks passing through people who are the eyes and ears on the ground. But it also ushered in the advent of new technology. Wiretaps were common, bugging phones and rooms with eavesdropping equipment, and eventually the advent of spy planes and satellite intelligence that could read the license plate of a car from outer space became more than just fiction.

THE WORLD'S SECOND-OLDEST PROFESSION

The Cold War was fought primarily in darkness, relying on information of what the other side was doing. There is a tongue-in-cheek saying that the United States "collects intelligence"—the *other side* does that dastardly "spying." The spy is the smallest and single most important unit of warfare. The first account of spies is found in the Bible. For those who fell asleep during Bible study, here are passages found in the Old Testament.[18] As a bonus, we are treated to the first use of a "safe house," a location often used to debrief for information culled during a mission.

> *The Lord said to Moses, "Send men to explore Canaan, which I'm giving to the Israelites. Send one leader from each of their ancestors' tribes."*
>
> *So at the Lord's command, Moses sent these men from the Desert of Paran. All of them were leaders of the Israelites…*

When Moses sent them to explore Canaan, he told them, "Go through the Negev and then into the mountain region. See what the land is like and whether the people living there are strong or weak, few or many. Is the land they live in good or bad? Do their cities have walls around them or not? Is the soil rich or poor? Does the land have trees or not? Do your best to bring back some fruit from the land."

After forty days, these men returned and reported their findings, making this the oldest reported spy mission in the world—on record as the world's second-oldest profession. As we can see from this Bible lesson, it suggests that the occupation of a spy was a creation from God.

Here is another passage:

Then Joshua, son of Nun secretly sent two spies from Shittim. "Go, look over the land," he said, "especially Jericho." So they went and entered the house of a prostitute named Rahab and stayed there.

The king of Jericho was told, "Look, some of the Israelites have come here tonight to spy out the land." So the king of Jericho sent this message to Rahab: "Bring out the men who came to you and entered your house, because they have come to spy out the whole land."

But the woman had taken the two men and hidden them. She said, "Yes, the men came to me, but I did not know where they had come from. At dusk, when it was time to close the city gate, they left. I don't know which way they went. Go after them quickly. You may catch up with them."

Thus, the world's second-oldest profession was born.

ROBERT HANSSEN: COLD WAR BETRAYAL OF AMERICA

Robert Hanssen was born as an only child to Howard and Vivian Hanssen in the Norwood Park neighborhood of Chicago on April 18, 1944. Howard was serving as a petty officer in the navy during the Second World War when Robert was born. Howard was a Chicago police officer, and right before Robert joined the force, Howard was a district commander in Norwood Park, which was closest to home to be with his family.

Despite having a difficult relationship with his father, Robert Hanssen followed Howard's footsteps in the Chicago Police Department in October

1972 a few months after Howard retired from the force. During his tenure in the department, Robert was assigned to the surveillance unit working to ferret out the corruption of other police officers, despite his not having ever worked as a beat cop.

Howard had always wanted his son to be a doctor. Robert obliged at least partially by enrolling in Dental School at Northwestern University after attending undergraduate school at Knox College in Galesburg, Illinois. After finishing dental school, Robert decided to venture into business education and earned an MBA and CPA. He desired a position in the National Security Agency but was rejected. Soon thereafter, he took a position in countersurveillance with the Federal Bureau of Investigation.

Like Father, Like Son

Surveillance ran in the family with both Robert and his father. Howard became involved in the notorious Chicago Red Squad during the 1950s and '60s, undertaken by Mayor Richard Daley, which resulted in unapproved methods to infiltrate and use illegal domestic surveillance on elements of the city considered aggressively dangerous, communist and socialist in nature. In the 1960s, the Peace Movement evolved into wide-ranging protests against the war in Vietnam. Chicago was especially a hotbed of activity involving mostly peaceful demonstrations, but some incidents turned violent, including the Days of Rage in 1967. As protesters from Students for a Democratic Society (and later its splinter group the Weathermen) turned more violent, surveillance and informants were placed within those cells and gathered intelligence that could conceivably harm not just property but people. The Weathermen especially were linked to violent methods, having taken credit for blowing up the Pentagon and Capitol Building in Washington, D.C., and many other targets, including a monument to police officers in recognition of their work against the Haymarket Affair rioters in 1886.

Red Squads were in full use in larger police departments in Chicago, Los Angeles and New York City. Surveillance methods against anarchist and militant labor unions in Chicago were present as early as the Haymarket Affair in 1886. In 1904, New York City undertook increased watchfulness, with Italian immigrants suspected as members of gangs and the mob. Red Squads would turn their full attention to suspected communists starting in the 1930s as Stalin tightened his grip in Russia and kept full rein on organizations such as the Communist Party USA.

These surveillance methods and intrusions into civilian lives had taken their course during the Vietnam War–era protests. In 1974, Howard Hanssen was involved in a suspicious fire in the records room of the police department. The fire broke out in the area where files were housed, and the scenario itself became suspicious when only the file cabinets that housed Red Squad materials and investigations caught fire (none of the adjacent files was touched).

Robert Hanssen's Career with the FBI

As Hanssen's stint with the Chicago Police Department drew to a close in 1975, he was offered a job with counterintelligence at the FBI. He was assigned to the Midwest office of the FBI located in Gary, Indiana. Looking for a bigger assignment, Hanssen was eventually transferred to the New York City branch in 1979, where he developed the first counterintelligence database for the FBI. Just eight months after his position in New York City, he delivered a package to the GRU, the military espionage wing of the Soviet Union. Having known all of the technological equipment and methods of the FBI, plus working as an accountant as CPA, Hanssen would go nearly undetected until his arrest in 2001. He was arrested just two months shy of his mandatory retirement date.[19]

A damning conclusion of Robert Hanssen's activities was found in "A Review of the FBI's Performance in Deterring, Detecting, and Investigating the Espionage Activities of Robert Philip Hanssen," compiled by the Office of the Inspector General in August 2003. Hanssen's espionage spanned three separate periods: 1979–81, 1985–91 and 1999–2001.[20] Over more than twenty years, Hanssen compromised some of this nation's most important counterintelligence and military secrets, including the identities of dozens of human sources, at least three of whom were executed. Hanssen gave the KGB thousands of pages of highly classified documents and dozens of computer disks detailing U.S. strategies in the event of nuclear war, major developments in military weapons technologies, information on active espionage cases and many other aspects of the U.S. Intelligence Community's Soviet counterintelligence program. In 1979, his wife, Bonnie, noticed him writing letters in his den. Assuming it was an affair, she confronted Robert about the infidelity. Little did she expect to hear that he was actually spying against the United States government. He went to confession as early as 1980 to admit to his espionage. Since

FBI agent Robert Hanssen.

clergy are by no means required to report the confession to the authorities, it went unknown for decades.

In the early 1980s, Hanssen served in the Budget Unit and in the Soviet Analytical Unit at FBI Headquarters, positions that provided him with broad access to sensitive information and an opportunity to use his technical and computer skills but did not require operational work. Because the Budget Unit was responsible for preparing materials justifying the FBI's budget requests to Congress, Hanssen obtained access to sensitive information from all components of the Intelligence Division and worked closely with the NSA and the CIA to secure joint funding for certain projects. In the Soviet Analytical Unit, Hanssen gained access to the FBI's most sensitive human assets and technical operations against the Soviet Union. He also began a noticeable pattern of mishandling classified information, primarily by disclosing the existence of Soviet sources and investigations to people with no "need to know," such as FBI employees in other divisions and personnel from other agencies. While Hanssen's tours in the Budget and Soviet Analytical Units showed that he was an intelligent, analytical agent with significant computer skills, his performance also revealed that he lacked the interpersonal skills to communicate effectively and perform supervisory duties. Nonetheless, Hanssen's career at the FBI continued to advance.

In 1985, Hanssen returned to the New York office as the supervisor of a technical surveillance squad. Hanssen was a lackadaisical manager who did not interact effectively with his subordinates. Because the squad largely "ran itself," however, Hanssen's limited interpersonal skills did not become a significant issue. Similarly, Hanssen's mishandling of classified information was obvious to his subordinates but was not brought to the attention of his superiors.

1985: Year of the Spy

Hanssen had paused his espionage activities, restarting in 1985, the same year that multiple high-level traitors offered their services to the Soviet

Union. John Walker was apprehended for sending naval information to the Soviets for nearly eighteen years. Jonathon Pollack provided information to the KGB, insisting that the information would assist Israel. Perhaps the most notorious, Aldrich Ames, also offered his services as a CIA officer to the Soviets. Robert Hanssen would return to this world, while others gave invaluable information that put countless agents working both for the United States and against the Cold War enemy of the Soviet Union in danger. Hanssen pled guilty to fifteen counts of espionage in 2001. He was sentenced to life in prison without any chance of parole.

Aldrich Ames in a high school photo.

WERNER JURETZKO: THE SPY NEXT DOOR

In 1945, Werner Juretzko found himself a teenage boy conscripted into the local Hitler Youth in an area of Soviet-occupied Poland. He and his group were ordered to dig trenches to protect against the rapidly advancing Soviet army near his home in the oft-disputed region of Upper Silesia. Called on to halt the advance from the east, Werner and others in the Hitler Youth brigade were the remaining few of the forces of lines protecting German-occupied territory from the Soviet advance. Sensing his demise and taking advantage of an opportunity to escape, Werner, along with his sister, Frieda, trekked west to find safety out of the Soviet-occupied areas of Central Europe. They were quickly apprehended by Soviet occupation soldiers and impounded until the war concluded. Werner became a prisoner of war and was held captive for several months in the Soviet-Czech POW camp located in Tabor, Czechoslovakia, as the Second World War ended. Frieda was harassed, raped and would die due to the actions of ruthless Soviet soldiers. Throughout this ordeal, Werner carried an internal hatred of the Soviet Union and its subsequent occupation of Germany. Atrocities committed by Soviet soldiers against members of his family created a resolve in Werner to avenge his family's honor. The activist path that he chose was exemplified by his intelligence gathering work for the Western world behind the Iron Curtain during the Cold War years of the late 1940s and 1950s.

In 1946, Werner fled the area of Soviet-occupied Poland, trying to make his way to the West. He was fearful of arrest due to his outspoken anti-communist beliefs. He landed by train in the town of Kassel in the American zone, where he found a job as an apprentice in a heavy machinery plant. The German Communist Party's agitation and propaganda apparatus were in high gear at the time, trying to organize the plant's workers, with little success. Juretzko's outspoken opposition soon drew the attention of the local criminal investigation section charged with combating political extremism of both right and left. He became an undercover operative and was instructed to change his view on communism—at least in public. The local communists would accept the new convert.

One of his first high-profile assignments was joining a peace group supported by East Germany and the communist Free German Youth, both of which were virulently anti-American. Among his duties in the so-called peace movement was to "ask" local businesses for "donations" to peaceful causes such as dispensing with Western presence in Germany, as well as those efforts to support comrades fighting inside the Korean peninsula, caused by "aggressive imperialists." Among Werner's other activities was to ignite passions against the American occupation of Berlin by slashing tires, placing graffiti in public places and fomenting anti-American and Western animosity in general. Internally, however, Werner kept police informed on upcoming demonstrations and the methods used by the East Germans to ship propaganda material to the West. United States G-2 military intelligence, which maintained a close liaison with the German police, liked Juretzko's diligence and recruited him as an agent in 1953. Juretzko kept his job as a master machinist, working to maintain a plausible identity to continue obtaining information and sources from the communist side.

Joining the Gehlen Organization

During the latter stages of the Second World War, German general Reinhard Gehlen was transferred to the G-2 army intelligence unit. Gehlen had been the head of Hitler's intelligence on the Eastern Front. The United States needed intelligence of Soviet and Soviet-occupied sources. In exchange for his removal as a war criminal, General Gehlen would supply his valuable intelligence and maintain a network through 1955. One of those then recruited to take part in activities in 1953 was Werner Juretzko. Thus began a two-year stint working with the West during the early years of the Cold War. As a G-2 political undercover operative for U.S. Army Intelligence, Werner conducted authorized espionage missions behind the Iron Curtain. Werner would conduct missions of counting MiG 15 and MiG 17 Soviet fighter jets in airfields around Soviet/East German air force bases inside the Iron Curtain.

In early August 1955, Werner crossed through the Iron Curtain into East Germany on a bicycle. Werner is fond of pointing out the differences between his espionage activities and that of the famous U-2 pilot Francis Gary Powers, shot down over the Soviet Union in 1960 and subsequently held prisoner. Powers was given control of a nearly $250 million U-2 aircraft, and Werner was given a 250 East German Mark bicycle. That seventh spy mission behind the Iron Curtain proved to be the unlucky final foray that doomed him. He was caught at a hotel in Schwerin, East Germany—eating what evidence he could to destroy his culpability. Werner Juretzko, however, barely twenty-three, was destined to be confined to a communist dungeon.

After his apprehension by the East German Stasi while on an authorized mission in 1955, Werner was accused of, and tried for, anti-communist activities. He was tried and sentenced to thirteen years of incarceration for so-called crimes against the German Democratic Republic, Article 6 of its constitution. As a political prisoner, Werner spent six years of his imprisonment in the infamous underground torture chambers of the Stasi secret police in Berlin-Hohenschoenhausen, the notorious "Red Ox" in Halle and other barbaric, inhumane prisons such as the Brandenburg-Goerden penitentiary. As a formality, according to his handlers in the West, Agent Werner Markus (aka Stanislaw Sowboda) failed to make contact with the G-2 organization on September 15, 1955, and was considered lost to the enemy. His action was taken by G-2 without prejudice, and in explanation, G-2 stated that the agent failed to maintain contact with G-2.

Serving His Prison Sentence

In October 1946, the KGB established an underground central detainment prison located at Hohenschoenhausen in East Berlin. Werner described his isolation and the prison techniques of torture. One section of cells that lacked daylight was known to prisoners, guards and administrators alike as the "U-Boat" (named after the German submarine). His treatment as prisoner of the East German state included physical violence and psychological torture, including being forced to stand and water cells. Disorientation, isolation, cold, heat, water and noise cells, along with a diet consisting solely of salty foods with the absence of water, were also implemented during Werner's prison sentence. These were the most common physical tortures.

Werner recounted his worst day in prison, most notably the stress of what determination would be made regarding a death sentence or lengthy prison term. During the last days of November 1955, this underground KGB/Stasi interrogation cell in East Berlin held two men: Heinz Friedemann and Werner Juretzko. Only one of them would leave this Stasi prison cell alive. Werner was the fortunate one.

Prisoners Nos. 12-2 and 12-3

From here, prisoner no. 12-2 and British spy no. 554, Heinz Friedemann, was led to the guillotine and beheaded on December 22, 1955. The condemned was notified that his petition for mercy had been denied and that the execution would be carried out during the morning hours of December 22. The condemned remained calm in the face of this announcement, and when asked, he begged to be allowed to write to his family and to smoke. He also begged for something to eat. All his wishes were granted. The condemned spent the night smoking and writing. He kept calm all night and caused no problems. At 0255 hours, he was shackled and led into the execution room. There, in the presence of three comrades from the Stasi-Berlin and Dr. Skrobeck, chief medical examiner, as well as the warden, the verdict was briefly announced once more. Thereafter, he was handed over to the executioner. The execution lasted only about two seconds. On his death certificate, Friedemann's cause of death was listed as heart failure.

Prisoner no. 12-3, G-2 United States Army Intelligence operative Werner Juretzko, received a sentence of thirteen years and was transported to a maximum-security prison. Werner learned of his fate while being summoned to meet his interrogator. Instead of meeting his usual interrogator, however, he saw the largest human being he had ever met. Due to this Stasi officer's large hands, Werner assumed that he would meet his fate at the hands of a choker and be killed on the spot. Instead, he learned of a long prison sentence. By his own account, Werner was thrown into an underground prison for stretches in solitary confinement without a gleam of daylight. He began a thirteen-year sentence that seemed like several lifetimes, stretched end to end, all terminated by new terror through punishment and interrogation—started anew by entry into one of the sixty-eight underground cells that had become the main interrogation prison of East Germany's State Security Police.

During his stay in various prisons, Werner shared his cell with a variety of prisoners of the former Wehrmacht, KGB/Stasi and East German prisoners and prisoners from other Iron Curtain countries. While communicating through the walls, he learned of a woman named Elli Barczatis. Werner was not aware of who Barczatis was at the time of his internment. In retrospect, she turned out to be the secretary to East German prime minister Otto Grotewohl; Barczatis had been passing secrets to the West. During the time of his imprisonment, Werner was very aware that a guillotine awaited her as part of a death sentence. Upon his release, Werner would tell his debriefers of the guillotine being used to execute prisoners of the East German state. In a state of disbelief, his debriefers had replied to Werner that he was not sent to the era of the French Revolution, as the guillotine was no longer used.

Returning after six years and two weeks from East Germany, stepping on Western soil again, Werner filed a two-word report with his debriefers: "Mission Accomplished." Werner eventually made his way to Chicago, studied engineering and went back into the machining occupation. For years, he would not discuss his background. Once the Berlin Wall fell, Werner made his way back to Berlin and demanded his and other prisoner records from the Stasi.

Major General Gerhard Niebling, deputy defense minister and coauthor of the 4+2 German unification treaty after the collapse of the German Democratic Republic, had been Friedemann's interrogator. Werner Juretzko filed murder charges against him after the fall of the Berlin Wall. When interviewed by a reporter of the *Berliner Post* about how he felt in light of Juretzko's charges, he replied, "I believe Juretzko is reading too many western detective stories!"

The cell door in Hohenschoenhausen prison, behind which Werner Juretzko and John Van Altena served prison time in East Germany, is adjacent to the one depicted in the 2015 movie *Bridge of Spies*, starring Tom Hanks and directed by Steven Spielberg. In the movie, Tom Hanks's character, John Donovan, is placed in custody overnight while traveling inside East Berlin to negotiate the release of U-2 pilot Francis Gary Powers.

The Stasi prison cell door in the Safe House in Milwaukee was visited by two notable Soviets. Sergei Khrushchev, son of Soviet leader Nikita Khrushchev, was one such dignitary. Sergei was a guest of the Cold War Museum Midwest Chapter in 2006, cosponsored by the Safe House. A few years later, KGB general Oleg Kalugin visited the Safe House while in town giving a talk to the FBI. Oleg Kalugin was the highest-ranking KGB defector to the United States. Kalugin (a counterintelligence agent and one-time superior to Vladimir Putin) and former prisoner Werner Juretzko stood in front of the cell door, discussing times past, as they were foes during the Cold War era. In a twist of destiny, both Sergei Khrushchev and Oleg Kalugin became United States citizens. These two former enemies of the United States, sworn to uphold the laws of the Soviet Union, became citizens of the nation they had vowed to destroy.

EAST GERMAN STASI PRISONER REUNION

Francis Gary Powers Jr. was extended an invitation to a lecture on behalf of a local Cold War history group formed in 2003. Gary was the founder of the Cold War Museum in Washington, D.C. The founding of the museum was intended to honor his father's Cold War legacy as a U-2 pilot shot down over the Soviet Union in 1960, subsequent imprisonment and release in exchange for Soviet colonel Rudolf Abel. The movie *Bridge of Spies*, directed by Steven Spielberg and starring Tom Hanks as John Donovan, who arranged the famous spy swap in 1962, gives a handy account of the story. In order to recognize the heretofore unheralded stories of the Cold War era, the mission of the Cold War Museum expanded broadly to include several decades' worth of conflict with the Soviet Union. Gary Powers' invite spurred coordination of efforts and creation of the Midwest Chapter of the Cold War Museum.

My former school teacher John Van Altena and I reconnected shortly before Gary's visit, and he and I discussed his Cold War history in East German Stasi prisons in the early 1960s. The Stasi was the East German secret police that kept that government's control over the population during the Cold War. Fortunately, John had written a book, *A Guest of the State*, in 1968 that recounted John's capture, foray into the Stasi prison system and eventual release. It was said that at any given time, the Stasi convinced one out of every sixty-seven people to become informants. Under communism, it was very lucrative to give information to the state to get ahead. That might include a better job, a larger flat (apartment), more rations and luxuries such as a television, a washing machine or even a vehicle. The ability to snitch on a family member, neighbor, co-worker, boss or other resident created an aura of suspicion that formed the basis of distrust among the population.

A surprise reunion took place due to the invitation of Gary Powers to lecture in Waukesha, Wisconsin. Gary had given me a contact in Chicago named Werner Juretzko to invite to his lecture at Carroll University while he was town. Werner had a peculiar past, as discussed previously. Talking by telephone with Werner, in his thick German accent, he was shaken upon my mention of John Van Altena's name. Werner had not seen John since 1968, some thirty-six years prior. Both Werner and John had shared a history at East Berlin's notorious Hohenschoenhausen prison during the Cold War, albeit at different times and for different reasons. Werner served a stretch of time in the notorious prison from 1955 to 1961 for crimes against the state of East Germany. John and Werner had met by happenstance during John's book tour in 1968. Thereafter, they would visit each other's homes to share stories. Werner, a Chicagoan since 1962, when he immigrated to the United States, was invited to John's farm in Wisconsin and recalled an amusing scenario visiting an American farm for the first time. As a city dweller, Werner was in need of farm attire and showed up to John's farm wearing boots, expecting to walk through cow manure. His first impression was memorable in that Werner walked inside the farmhouse and saw only books.[20] Werner's immediate thought was that John and his family must have been book farmers! Nonetheless, the Francis Gary Powers event with Werner and John was a reunion taken right out of the annals of *This Is Your Life*—rather astonishing given the short notice.

THE WORLD OF JAMES BOND: OFFICIAL AUTHOR RAYMOND BENSON

Chicago-area resident Raymond Benson was sitting around a table with friends in 1981 and discussing what it is that they would write if given the chance. Benson indicated a bedside compendium of James Bond information in a handy format as a coffee table book. His friends were in agreement that it would make wonderful copy. Through a mutual friend, an editor was contacted, and the process to write it was underway, with a contract offered. It took three years to research and put it into a final format. Raymond went to visit the Ian Fleming estate in England, talking with friends and family of the late author to glean information for his book. The book was published in 1984 and nominated for the Edgar Allan Poe Award for Best Biographical/

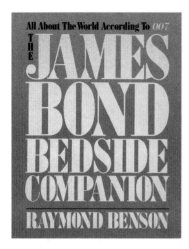

Top: *James Bond Bedside Companion.*
Courtesy of Raymond Benson.

Bottom: Raymond Benson with
"Q," Desmond Llewelyn. *Courtesy of*
Raymond Benson.

Critical Work. The book was updated in 1988 to account for the British audience and to include Roger Moore's final film, *A View to a Kill*, and Timothy Dalton's first appearance, the film *The Living Daylights*.[21]

While growing up in Odessa, Texas, in the 1960s, Raymond was smitten by the *Goldfinger* vinyl soundtrack, which his next-door neighbors played continually. His father finally took him to see the *Goldfinger* movie, and Raymond took in all things Bond thereafter. The double feature of *Dr. No* and *From Russia with Love* in 1966 further cemented his love of James Bond adventure and lore. He read the Ian Fleming books and followed the franchise religiously, a series that would be matched in tenacity only when *Star Wars* burst onto the film scene in 1977.

Continuing to follow Bond throughout the 1970s and '80s, Raymond did not quit his "day job" by any means and enjoyed pursuits writing computer games after publication of the *James Bond Bedside Companion*. Games at that time were in text format and involved solving puzzles or going on journeys or quests. Raymond then ventured into writing for the James Bond franchise. In 1985, Raymond worked as a designer and writer on the computer game *James Bond 007: A View to a Kill*. He followed this in 1986 with work on a computer game version of *Goldfinger* and coauthoring the *You Only Live Twice II* module of the popular role-playing game *James Bond 007*.

He continued in the computer game industry for the largest computer game company in the world at the time and had a stint working for Viacom New Media in 1993, when settling into Chicago suburbs for the company. In 1995, he received a call from Glidrose Publications after the British writer

John Gardner had retired from penning the James Bond novels. Gardner had been the author of fourteen Bond novels and two film novelizations (*GoldenEye* and *A License to Kill*).

The choosing of an American author, rather than a traditional English author, was met with some criticism, but Raymond would win over fans of James Bond with six novels, three movie novelizations (*Tomorrow Never Dies, The World Is Not Enough* and *Die Another Day*) and three short stories. Coincidentally, the computer gaming company Raymond worked for went out of business in 1997, a timely transition to writing the Bond series. Raymond would write from 1997 to 2002. Among his post-Bond run of writing, Raymond would write five titles in the Black Stiletto series, with an adapted series in preproduction with actress Mila Kunis since 2015.[22]

CHAPTER 5

DAWN OF THE ATOMIC AGE

MANHATTAN PROJECT IN CHICAGO

The Manhattan Project brought together the world's most foremost scientists in an effort to create a weapon more powerful than mankind had ever seen. There was great fear that Nazi Germany was also undertaking efforts to create this super weapon, created by nuclear fission of particles. What resulted was an atomic bomb that was dropped on Japan not once but twice in the span of a few days in August 1945, first over Hiroshima and then in Nagasaki, until the Japanese formally surrendered on September 2, 1945. The date was almost exactly six years after Germany—followed by the Soviet Union—invaded Poland, beginning on September 1, 1939. More than 70 million people are estimated to have perished as a result of the Second World War, which concluded in 1945.

In order to bring the war to a close faster, especially to save more lives and resources, work was feverishly undertaken to develop the bomb. J. Robert Oppenheimer and General Leslie Groves were selected to oversee the massive undertaking from both civilian and military standpoints. Research and production took place at more than thirty sites across the United States, the United Kingdom and Canada. Most notable were the laboratories at Los Alamos, New Mexico, and Oak Ridge, Tennessee. Another was at the University of Chicago, led by physicists Enrico Fermi and Leo Szilard. It would become the sight of the world's first man-made nuclear reactor in 1942.

LETTER TO THE PRESIDENT FROM ALBERT EINSTEIN

One month before the invasion of Poland by Nazi Germany and the Soviet Union, Albert Einstein was prompted to write a letter to Franklin Delano Roosevelt espousing the promise of nuclear fission in the development of an atomic bomb. Written by Szilard in consultation with fellow Hungarian physicists Edward Teller and Eugene Wigner, the letter warned that Germany might develop atomic bombs and suggested that the United States should start its own nuclear program. Two more letters promoting nuclear research would follow. The first letter by Szilard and signed by Einstein read as follows:

Old Grove Rd.
Nassau Point
Peconic, Long Island
August 2nd, 1939

F.D. Roosevelt,
President of the United States,
White House
Washington, D.C.

Sir:
Some recent work by E. Fermi and L. Szilard, which has been communicated to me in manuscript, leads me to expect that the element uranium may be turned into a new and important source of energy in the immediate future. Certain aspects of the situation which has arisen seem to call for watchfulness and, if necessary, quick action on the part of the Administration. I believe therefore that it is my duty to bring to your attention the following facts and recommendations:

In the course of the last four months it has been made probable—through the work of Joliot in France as well as Fermi and Szilard in America—that it may become possible to set up a nuclear chain reaction in a large mass of uranium by which vast amounts of power and large quantities of new radium-like elements would be generated. Now it appears almost certain that this could be achieved in the immediate future.

This phenomenon would also lead to the construction of bombs, and it is conceivable—though much less certain—that extremely powerful bombs of a new type may thus be constructed. A single bomb of this type, carried by boat and exploded in a port, might very well destroy the whole port together with some of the surrounding territory. However, such bombs might very well prove to be too heavy for transportation by air.

The United States has only very poor ores of uranium in moderate quantities. There is some good ore in Canada and the former Czechoslovakia, while the most important source of uranium is Belgian Congo.

In view of this situation you may think it desirable to have some permanent contact maintained between the Administration and the group of physicists working on chain reactions in America. One possible way of achieving this might be for you to entrust with this task a person who has your confidence and who could perhaps serve in an unofficial capacity. His task might comprise the following:

a) to approach Government Departments, keep them informed of the further development, and put forward recommendations for Government action, giving particular attention to the problem of securing a supply of uranium ore for the United States.

b) to speed up the experimental work, which is at present being carried on within the limits of the budgets of University laboratories, by providing funds, if such funds be required, through his contacts with private persons who are willing to make contributions for this cause, and perhaps also by obtaining the co-operation of industrial laboratories which have the necessary equipment.

I understand that Germany has actually stopped the sale of uranium from the Czechoslovakian mines which she has taken over. That she should have taken such early action might perhaps be understood on the ground that the son of the German Under-Secretary of State, von Weizsäcker, is attached to the Kaiser-Wilhelm-Institut in Berlin where some of the American work on uranium is now being repeated.

Yours very truly,
Albert Einstein[23]

Chicago Pile at Stagg Field, 1942.

In December 1942, under the stands of Stagg Field at the University of Chicago, Enrico Fermi and Leo Szilard initiated the first human-controlled atomic chain reaction in history. Thus began the Atomic Age. The reactor, Chicago Pile One (CP-1), was later rechristened the CP-2 and moved to nearby Palos Park as part of the Manhattan Project. A second reactor, the CP-3, was also built there. After the war, waste from and parts of both reactors were buried there; the dumpsite area is now part of the Palos Hills Forest Preserve.[24]

During the first half of 1942, Enrico Fermi and his S-1 team continued their efforts to construct an "atomic pile" where a chain reaction could be started. They began by building some small experimental piles. As the nuclear reaction project moved forward, more scientists took part. These included chemists, biologists, chemical engineers, metallurgists and engineers. Because of the known risks to the people who worked with radioactive materials, health researchers were recruited to take part as well. Besides the uranium that would create the chain reaction, the team needed large amounts of pure graphite. This material, which would surround the uranium and help obtain the reaction, was a necessary ingredient to testing the reaction. In total, forty tons of graphite were ordered for the experiments on atomic piles.

After experimenting with more than thirty piles, the group sought out a safe, secret place for its nuclear reactor and chose the squash court under Stagg Field Stadium on the University of Chicago campus. In November, the construction began in earnest. Graphite bricks were made by skilled mechanics, with the black graphite dust clinging to their hands and clothing as they worked. One of these mechanics stated that the workers found out how coal miners felt, with the pores of their skin oozing dust despite taking a shower. When completed, the pile stood twenty six feet tall and required 380 tons of purified graphite, along with twenty-two thousand pellets of uranium. Total reactor cost in 1942 was $2.7 million (approximately $42 million in 2019 dollars).

December 2, 1942, was a bitterly cold winter day in Chicago. Inside the squash court, a group of about fifty people began gathering, including the scientists and builders of the reaction pile. Instruments were placed at specific spots throughout the pile to record the activity of the neutrons passing through. In a humorous touch to the coming event, the instruments were named Piglet, Roo, Kanga and Tigger—named after the *Winnie the Pooh* characters. Enrico Fermi had been reading a children's book to improve his English.[25]

The outcome was less than certain, and those present had a high probability of dying from radiation poisoning and or an explosion. An explosion of uranium would be especially dangerous to those on the University of Chicago campus and surrounding areas. When the rods were released from the pile, the Geiger counter measurements shot off the charts. As the experiment continued throughout the day, the reaction was

Squash court under Stagg Field.

contained. Finally, the moment emerged whereby Fermi closed his slide rule and declared to the group that a chain reaction had been self-sustaining. The reaction continued for twenty-eight minutes. The physicist Arthur Compton stated that a new age had begun, unleashing "the vast reserves of energy held in the nucleus of the atom were at the disposal of man."

A NOTABLE SPY INFILTRATES THE MANHATTAN PROJECT: KLAUS FUCHS

Despite unprecedented security on the Manhattan Project, the Soviets were still able to infiltrate the massive undertaking. The most influential of the atomic spies was Klaus Fuchs. Fuchs, a German-born British physicist, went to the United States to work on the atomic project and became one of its lead scientists. Fuchs had become a member of the Communist Party in 1932 while still a student in Germany. At the onset of the Third Reich in 1933, Fuchs fled to Great Britain. He eventually became one of the lead nuclear physicists in the British program. In 1943, he moved to the United States to collaborate on the Manhattan Project. Due to Fuchs's position in the atomic program, he had access to most, if not all, of the material Moscow desired. Fuchs was also able to interpret and understand the information he was stealing, which made him an invaluable resource. Fuchs provided the Soviets with detailed information on the gas-phase separation process. He also provided specifications for the payload, calculations and relationships for setting of the fission reaction and schematics for labs producing weapons-grade isotopes. This information helped the smaller, undermanned and undersupplied Soviet group move toward the successful detonation of a nuclear weapon.

The Soviet nuclear program would have eventually been able to develop a nuclear weapon without the aid of espionage. But it did not develop a basic understanding of the usefulness of an atomic weapon, the sheer resources required and the talent until much later. Espionage helped the Soviet scientists identify which methods worked and prevented their wasting valuable resources on techniques that the development of the American bomb had proven ineffective. The speed at which the Soviet nuclear program achieved a working bomb, with so few resources, depended on the amount of information acquired through espionage. During the Cold War trials, the United States emphasized the significance of that espionage. After a prison sentence, Fuchs would return to East Germany a hero and assist with the Soviet nuclear program.

Once the Soviets detonated their first atomic bomb in 1949, the Arms Race was underway. With the help of spies such as Klaus Fuchs during the Second World War—along with many other spies, informants and even couriers—the Soviets were able to detonate their atomic bomb well ahead of schedule. The West suffered an additional blow when communist forces under Mao Zedong took control of China after chasing the nationalist government of Chiang Kai-shek into Taiwan. Along with the fall of China and subsequent invasion by North Korea into South Korea, the Soviet atomic breakthrough pushed the existing world order into a frenzy.

Edward Teller, who figured prominently in the Chicago pile in 1942, advocated for a more powerful weapon in the hydrogen bomb, which would be detonated by the United States successfully in 1952. The Soviets would follow with their own test in 1955. Nuclear warheads were placed on missiles for land, air and sea. Atomic bombs were made smaller, larger and more powerful than the previous generation. Use of atomic bombs were even considered to lift spacecraft, having seen Project Orion operate for decades until the 1970s.

Eventually, there were efforts to curtail the Arms Race by both superpowers. There was widespread sentiment that weapons should not fall into the hands of rogue actors and that accidental launching of weapons should be avoided at all costs. Atomic testing taking place underground, in open air, on land and underwater was prohibited by the Partial Nuclear Test Ban Treaty, signed in 1963. A Strategic Arms Limitation Treaty (SALT) was undertaken by the United States and the USSR beginning in 1972. Detente, or the thawing of relations between Cold War adversaries, was a foreign policy solution sought by President Richard Nixon and advisor Henry Kissinger. Detente would allow the Americans to pursue relations with the Soviets and also the Chinese, thereby triangulating the communist adversaries at the same time. A second limitation treaty was signed by Jimmy Carter and Leonid Brezhnev.

In contrast to his predecessors, Ronald Reagan had a vision of reducing nuclear weapons, as opposed to simply limiting them under the SALT treaties. An intermediate-range nuclear weapons reduction treaty was signed by both Reagan and Mikhail Gorbachev in 1988. START (Strategic Arms Reduction Treaty) was initiated by President Ronald Reagan and signed by his successor, George H.W. Bush, in 1991.

NUCLEAR HISTORY OF ILLINOIS

Illinois was home to the first large-scale commercial power reactor, Unit 1 at the Commonwealth Edison's Dresden Power Station, opened in 1960. Subsequent serious radioactive contamination problems forced the permanent shutdown of this unit in 1978, thus also making it one of the first commercial power reactors to close prematurely.

Commonwealth Edison's two large Pressurized Water Reactors in Zion, Illinois, first opened in 1973, also had to close prematurely. They are the second- and third-largest (more than one thousand megawatts) power reactors to close prematurely, going offline in 1998.

Illinois also has the first and only commercial storage facility for high-level radioactive waste (HLRW), the General Electric Morris

Operation (GEMO). GEMO was to have operated as a spent nuclear fuel reprocessing facility, but the technology employed by GE was faulty and failed. The HLRW initially gathered to be reprocessed has largely remained at the site to this day.

Besides the three reactors that closed prematurely, Illinois currently has eleven operating nuclear reactors—far more than any other state.[26]

COULD A SIMILAR CHERNOBYL INCIDENT OCCUR IN ILLINOIS?

Overall, nuclear power has been proven to be a safe, clean technology while operational. The aftereffects of what to do with spent fuel rods in Illinois and other areas of the United States and the world will continue to present challenges for safety and ecological concerns. There are certainly hazards that have proven destructive, such as the Fukushima accident in Japan in 2011, and other close calls, such as Three Mile Island in Pennsylvania in 1979. To be sure, the design flaws in the Chernobyl nuclear plants, along with the de-emphasis of safety versus output results, are not present in American nuclear reactors. The effects of the Chernobyl explosion and the surrounding exclusion zone may be harmful for large-scale habitation for up to twenty thousand years. Despite this, there continues to be people who have lived in the zone for decades without any issues. These individuals breathe the air, eat food grown in gardens and use water from the surrounding area. Due to human inactivity in the 2,600-square-mile exclusion zone, the area is also teeming with wildlife and forest growth, displaying its natural beauty. If a reactor were damaged in Illinois, it would affect a wide range of the region, including the surrounding states of Wisconsin, Michigan and Indiana.

CHAPTER 6

NUCLEAR MISSILES

PROTECTING ILLINOIS

CHICAGO'S DEFENSE RING

After the Second World War, more than two hundred Nike missile sites sprang up all over the United States to become the next generation of antiaircraft weapons to deter invasion by an enemy air force. The first-generation missile was the Nike Ajax, a conventional warhead that would soon be replaced by the Nike Hercules. The Nike Hercules missile was outfitted with a thirty-kiloton nuclear warheads, each with the strength of similar size and power of those dropped on Hiroshima and Nagasaki in Japan. The Nike sites had about thirty missiles on sites, with a dozen nuclear warheads on hand.

WHY NUCLEAR MISSILES IN ILLINOIS?

As the third-largest population center in the United States, Chicago was prime military target during the Cold War. Thus, the Greater Milwaukee/ Chicago/Gary, Indiana area was of importance for defense planning and missile placement. The metropolitan area was home to a large manufacturing base that was certain to become an industrial target in the event of a third world war breaking out between the Soviet Union and the United States during the Cold War. To the north, Wisconsin companies like Allis Chalmers,

AC Delco and International Harvester, buttressed by foundries and various factories, were prime targets as well.

The Greater Chicago area and region had multiple targets of interest outside the population center. The Caterpillar plant in Peoria, the Great Lakes Naval Base, nuclear power plants, a port/ rail junction and foundries and other factories. The Chrysler motor plant in Kenosha and General Motors production lines in Janesville were also of importance. As such, the metropolitan area was outfitted with twenty missile sites starting in 1954 and 1955.

These Nike missile locations in the Chicago and Northwest Indiana area[27] included:

- C-03, Montrose Harbor/Belmont Harbor, 1955–65 (Lincoln Park)
- C-32, Porter, Indiana, 1957–74 (Indiana Dunes Lakeshore offices)
- C-40, Burnham Park, Chicago, 1955–63 (McCormack Place Bird Sanctuary)
- C-41, Jackson Park, Chicago, 1955–71
- C-44, Hegewisch/Wolf Lake, Illinois, 1956–63
- C-45, Gary Municipal Airport, Indiana, 1957–60
- C-46, Munster, Indiana, 1957–74 (industrial park)
- C-47, South Haven/Wheeler, Indiana, 1956–74
- C-48, Gary, Indiana, 1957–1960
- C-49/50, Homewood, Illinois, 1957–1974
- C-51, Alsip, Illinois/Palos Heights, Illinois, 1956–63
- C-54, Orland Park, Illinois, 1955–61
- C-61, Willowbrook, Illinois/Darien, Illinois, 1955–68 (Parkhurst U.S. Army Reserve Center)
- C-70, Naperville, Illinois, 1956–63 (Nike Park Sports Complex)
- C-72, Addison, Illinois, 1957–74 (Addison Park District)
- C-80/81, Arlington Heights, Illinois, 1950–74 (golf course/ Army Reserve Center)
- C-84, Palatine, Illinois, 1956–63 (corporate offices)
- C-92/94, Vernon Hills, Illinois, 1955–63 (Vernon Hills Athletic Complex)
- C-93, Northfield/Skokie Lagoons Glencoe, Illinois, 1955–74
- C-98, Fort Sheridan, Illinois, 1954–63 (Fort Sheridan National Cemetery)

Nike Hercules missile.

The original Nike Ajax missile batteries were reduced to seven sites once the Nike Hercules replaced the Nike Ajax. A further four more missile sites were located in the St. Louis ring protecting Southern Illinois region from Soviet bomber attack. They were under the command of Belleville AFS, which operated from 1959 to 1968, closing the Nike sites to which the batteries were purposed for:

- SL-10, Marine, Illinois, 1960–68
- SL-40, Hecker, Illinois, 1960–68
- SL-60, Pacific, Missouri, 1960–68
- SL-90, Alton/Pere Marquette May, Illinois, 1960–68 (Pere Marquette State Park)

The first-generation Nike Ajax missiles were conventional explosive warheads. The idea of these missiles was to come close to hitting approaching enemy Soviet bombers and damage the bombers before they inflicted damage on their targets. This meant destroying any portion of the aircraft as a means not necessarily of destruction but in taking the incoming aircraft off its trajectory and mission. By 1960, the next-generation Nike Hercules was beginning to phase out the conventional warheads and replace them with a nuclear warhead equivalent to those bombs dropped on Nagasaki and Hiroshima. The nuclear warhead was chosen because of its ability to knock out several incoming Soviet long-range bombers.

The Nike missiles were a last line of defense for those Soviet bombers. The missile sites were under control of the North American Air Defense Command (NORAD). The overall defense plan was to engage Soviet incursions into Canada, where the population was more sparsely populated, to minimize casualties. The Distant Early Warning Line (known as the DEW line), the Near Canada Line, followed by the Nike missile sites, would take their place as the last-ditch attempt to take out any remaining bombers. For these Chicago-area missiles, the radar would have picked up incoming bombers over Wisconsin, subsequently aiming and tracking toward those underpopulated areas. Consequently, missiles based in the Milwaukee area would point farther north. Nike veterans would remark that they might have barely launched two or three missiles, if they were lucky, before being taken out by Soviet aircraft.

During testing and training, Strategic Air Command (SAC) directed bombers in simulations over Nike missile sites. Nike veterans remarked that they had difficulty honing in on the aircraft with early radar systems, struggling to maintain a connection at 30 percent of simulation speeds for the bombers. Nike veterans also noted that there was nowhere to hide from the nuclear fallout that would have ensued after detonation in the skies over the area. If the bombers reached this far, they surmised, devastation was the only recourse for everyone.

RECALLING CHICAGO-AREA NIKE MISSILES

Marvin Rubenstein, who grew up in Chicago when the Nike missiles were present on the lakeshore, shared his memories of the sites that dotted the lakeshore. Marvin was the youngest of three college journalists credentialed by NASA to cover the Apollo 11 launch in 1969 (see chapter 9). Growing up in Chicago, he had little exposure to rocketry other than the Nike missile sites. He did, however, recall shooting plastic Nike models across the room using a spring launcher during his childhood. The model was provided as a toy prize in a box of Kellogg's Sugar Puffs.

At a young age, Marvin also understood Chicago's defensive importance as a Soviet target due to the city's abundance of manufacturing, steel industry, hub of transportation and large civilian population. History clearly was not lost on him. Within thirty-three blocks of his childhood home were Nike missiles aimed at shooting down long-range Russian bombers, along with Stagg Field—the site of Enrico Fermi's testing of the world's first atomic reaction in 1942 for the Manhattan Project (see chapter 5).

On Armed Forces Day each year, the Nike sites were opened to the public, and Marvin's father used the opportunity to take his family to the site at Jackson Park. Marvin vividly recalled several mounted missiles outside their underground pits on display at different angles. As he and his family were lowered to the missile pit storage area, the reality of the Cold War set in. Marvin felt awe seeing the missile and warhead adjacent to him.

FATE OF THE NIKE MISSILES

The Nike missile sites around the country had been largely shut down by 1971 under terms of the Strategic Arms Limitation Treaty. Sergei Khrushchev noted to me that his father, Nikita, was putting more emphasis on long-range intercontinental ballistic missiles (ICBMs). With the new threat and focus of these ICBMs by both sides, the Nike missile sites were rendered ineffective against that type of warfare weapon. A Nike Zeus missile was in development for years as a solution and deterrent to the ICBMs. But the Zeus was never fully deployed, falling out of favor for the Patriot missile in later years. Also factoring into the Nike missile's demise, the Vietnam War was taking up more manpower and resources; shutting down the Nike systems was an efficient decision compared to closing the bases outright.

The fate of the Nike missile sites varied by community. The sites were granted back to these various communities for development of parks and recreational purposes through the federal Department of the Interior via the National Park Service. Most Illinois Nike sites listed in this chapter have been repurposed as of this writing, noted in parentheses after their designation. Through its initial phase, then secretary of defense Donald Rumsfeld, who served under Presidents Richard Nixon and George W. Bush, was placed in charge of releasing the deeds to properties in Chicago and Northwest Indiana.

Chicago native Donald Rumsfeld would play a much larger role shaping U.S. defense policy, in addition to drawing down Nike missile bases across the country. As a Cold War veteran of the U.S. Navy, Rumsfeld was a naval aviator and trainer from 1954 to 1957. He was first elected to Congress in 1962 representing Illinois's Thirteenth District for three terms. He became a leading cosponsor of the Freedom of Information Act. After a stint in the Nixon administration, Rumsfeld became secretary of defense under Gerald Ford, the youngest in that position (1975–77) and later the second oldest under George W. Bush (2016).

The biggest challenge facing Rumsfeld's first stint was a transition from a draft-oriented military to one that was an all-volunteer service opportunity. Accordingly, defense budgets were being curtailed with the drawdown in forces in Southeast Asia and the end of hostilities in the Vietnam War. The B-1 Supersonic Lancer and cruise missile development became priorities under Rumsfeld's direction. Several months after his second tenure as secretary of defense, the September 11 attacks occurred. Rumsfeld would direct wars in Afghanistan in 2001 and Iraq in 2003. In 2001, a joint U.S. Air Force, U.S. Army and U.S. Marine Corps base was created at Karshi-Khanabad Air Base in Uzbekistan for use in the war in Afghanistan. The base was formerly an aviation regiment for Soviet Air Defense from 1950 to 1992, when the Soviet Union dissolved and it reverted back to Uzbeki control.

Undoubtedly, few people would be aware that nuclear missiles were once pointed at the skies for incoming Soviet nuclear bombers with the sole purpose of annihilating the Greater Chicago or St. Louis areas. Little remains of most of these sites, but if one looks closely enough, there are signs of Nike-era buildings and footprints of what was a massive defensive undertaking during the Cold War across the United States.

CHAPTER 7
EXILES

FLEEING STALIN'S TERROR

THE FORGOTTEN ODYSSEY OF POLISH CITIZENS
IN SOVIET CONTROLLED POLAND

I first met Wes Adamczyk at the American Polish Congress in Milwaukee in 2006. A vivid, disciplined speaker, Wes would remark that he didn't need notes, an outline in front of him or projected slides. With his graying hair tied in a ponytail, his delivery was remarkably crisp and pointed. The audience was mesmerized, listening intently to a topic obscure for many, including myself. Namely, Wes told how as a young boy he and his family were rounded up on trains in the middle of the night from eastern Poland and sent far away, to the barren steppes to the lands of Kazakhstan. In schools, students have been taught of the horrors Nazi Germany inflicted on untold millions, especially the Holocaust and rounding up of Jews all over Europe and Russia. The topic of the Second World War is also dominated by the rightful heroics of resistance fighters against Nazi Germany, tales of people like Anne Frank and her family hiding from the enemy and those who escaped the oncoming onslaught across the English Channel at Dunkirk. However, beginning with the invasion of Poland on September 1, 1939, there was another side to the fight from the Soviets. What seemed to be missing after all these years of learning the history of the Second World War was what happened on September 17, 1939. That story would unfold from the eastern side of Poland and involve exactly what Wes Adamczyk was relaying firsthand at the Polish Congress that evening.[28]

THE MOLOTOV–VON RIBBENTROP AGREEMENT

Earlier that summer, in 1939, a secret agreement took place whereby Germany and the Soviet Union would invade Poland and divide the land and spoils between themselves. The agreement also allowed a means for Stalin to continue making non-aggression pacts to stave off war for the USSR. Non-aggression pacts were plentiful between countries during the interwar period, an irony that would merely illustrate the façade of peace as the Second World War was on the horizon. Vladimir Lenin was quick to point out that soon after the ink dried, these types of agreements were useless, just as the vast amounts of currency the Bolsheviks printed off after assuming power become worthless instruments of purchasing power.

As the Soviets invaded from the east, soldiers pillaged, plundered and sought out anyone who might be challenge their power. Wes's father was a Polish military officer, so his family were targeted as immediate enemies. Wes's father was sent to the Russian front when hostilities broke out and was never heard from again. He remembered vividly his father's embrace as the family was left behind. His mother was left to care for older brother Jurek, sister Zosia and himself. They buried hunting guns in the backyard for fear of confiscation. When the knock came at the door to relocate the family to the east, Wes rued the guns buried and wished they could have been turned on these uncouth soldiers. "Citizen" was the preferred term of the Soviets, and when Wes addressed them as "mister," he was corrected that only bourgeois society used such vulgar terms. Equality among all comrades was the norm—"comrade" being a way for these Soviet leaders to convey that they had respect for their new prisoners. Yet pointing out the pathetic circumstances of all who "shared" the wants and needs of this new workers' paradise was forbidden, subject to arrest and deportation farther east to the work camps of Siberia.

The family was given a limited amount of time to gather a few belongings for an unknown destination east; they were told only that this new paradise would be plentiful. The train ride was a horror. Shoved into cattle cars with no space or heat and little ventilation was a nightmare. The toilet consisted of a hole in the side of the train car, and the sheer embarrassment of relieving oneself was overshadowed by the difficulty of squatting to defecate. In a rare moment of humor, an older Polish man on the train spoke of Soviet ingenuity on the placement of the latrine. Had it been created in the middle of the floor, the relief point would have been subject to collapse of the flooring by its users. The small nature of the hole also took into consideration the inability for prisoners to escape through such a tiny hatch. On the few occasions the prisoners were allowed to leave the train car, at random stops in the countryside, Wes noticed the trail of feces left on the tracks from passengers making the journey before them. Routinely, prisoners would try to make a break for it and were gunned down. Others were shot for no reason or out of minor inconveniences or boredom in the guards themselves. Several years of death and destruction would follow.

Exiting the trains at the stops also afforded limited opportunities to trade for food and clothing. Those without items to barter were left to beg. To their surprise, these begging prisoners were confronted by beggars inside the Soviet Union. What paradise was his arresting officers referring to when they were told of a world of plenty for those so fortunate to live under communism and Stalin?

Wes's family was left to settle in Kazakhstan. The barren landscape left nothing to the imagination—they were trapped in a strange and unforgiving place. The sky met the land well over the horizon, devoid of trees or wildlife. They were placed with another Kazakh family who at first appeared uncouth and dirty, with a language barrier and crowding into their home an uncomforting reality. Lice, bedbugs, hunger pangs and other sores were rampant and went without medicine. Fire would break out across the prairie, and the windstorms that swept up branches and other objects would cause bodily harm to those in their paths. The Adamczyks' would learn that the Kazakhs detested the Soviet Union with a passion as well and were very friendly and giving considering the circumstances. The Soviet commissar insisted that those who worked would be able to eat. Wes's job as a six-year-old was to pick up cow dung with his bare hands. The dung was used as a fuel source that would be baked in the sun and stored all winter long. Limited rations did not come close to meeting the family's needs.

When possible, Wes's mother, Anna, would improve their new circumstances as best she could. Of the items she kept for future use was a watch, later bartered for use of a horse and food by a local farmer. Anna boldly sought permission to move into town, but local commissars were loath to assist these new transplanted Poles in an expedited manner. The local secret police kept close tabs on the family as well—not only to ensure that they weren't trying to escape but also to monitor their communications with the locals. Giving accurate information on better living conditions in Poland was of high interest to the NKVD. The West, as propaganda from Stalin on down insisted, was a deplorable place to live. Only Stalin's gifts to the population would be considered such a blessing to those so fortunate to be there!

The family were eventually allowed to move into the city. There they lived with an older couple who were standoffish at first but tried to accommodate this new family as best they could. The wife was never one to talk; she only looked distantly out the window for hours at a time. The couple rarely spoke and ate dinner in absolute silence. Wes later learned that the woman's relatives had been taken away by the Bolsheviks and killed. It left an indelible mark of depression and sadness on her for the rest of her life. The husband eventually opened up to Wes while teaching him how to fish on the local pond. Wes had continued to keep hope that the family could return to Poland, to which the old man responded in a dour manner that nobody escapes the Soviet Union alive. The regime would rather shoot anyone daring to even express leaving such a place rather than allow them to go and relate the horrors and lifelessness that existed in the USSR. A bright spot occurred when Jurek found a job assisting at a slaughterhouse. The workers (and supervisors) often procured certain cuts of meat taken discreetly away from the view of others. As a result, the family ate the best they had eaten in many months.

When the Germans invaded the Soviet Union in June 1942, a miraculous occurrence freed the Poles. Stalin had agreed to allow the Poles free movement, as well as create a standing Polish army that would act as an alliance to fend off the advancing Nazi units. Wes and his family learned of this in a frightening way. A knock on the door in the middle of the night startled everyone in the dwelling. Jurek was asked to go with the NKVD men making a house call. Anna cried, feeling that Jurek would be taken away, never to be seen again like his father. When Jurek came back several hours later, he explained the conniving plot by the NKVD to enlist him in the Soviet army. Cunningly refusing, Jurek instead received word that the Polish army was being formed and that all Polish citizens would be freed. The news was met with skepticism by Anna, and although true, the obvious barriers to money, food or transportation became a reality. There was also a lack of cooperation with the local authorities to issue papers that proved their ability to move freely about the country. Instead, Anna took a gamble with the chaos consuming the country and made her way with Wes and his sister to board trains heading to Persia (modern-day Iran).

Anna guessed correctly. However, there was no rhyme or reason to train schedules or where they were (no maps were available to peruse), and again there was the lack of money or food. What greeted them was utter chaos, disease, poverty and often death. Polish citizens were aimlessly taking trains across the region. Some would stop to beg for food, money or clothing, obtain boiling water or stretch their legs, only to see the train taking off without them. Lifeless souls were greeted at every stop, with some left for dead and others looking as if death had already taken them, but they continued to move on. Eventually, the Adamcyk family would make their way to Iran. Sadly, Wes's mother Anna succumbed to illness shortly after arrival.

Anna sacrificed immensely for her children. After Wes's father left the family to be with his army unit, his mother made what preparations she could for an uncertain future. That included sewing jewelry into the hems of her dresses and coats and those of her daughter. She also baked jewelry into loaves of bread, which she dried to provide a lasting supply of food for the family. Her body was laid to rest at a cemetery in Iran.

Illness was rampant in the camps while Wesley was in Persia. He came down with malaria twice, scarlet fever, mumps and measles in Persia over three years. In 1943, word spread quickly of Germans finding thousands of Polish officers dead in mass graves in Katyn. More than twenty-two thousand Poles were found buried in the Katyn forest. Polish officers in particular had been shot or buried alive as the Soviet Union had invaded eastern Poland in 1939. This news was known specifically because Polish soldiers forming from those who had been shipped east on the trains had inquired about thousands of officers who should have been released as well. The Soviet government refused to answer to the fates of those officers.

After the war in Europe ended in May 1945, there was a bittersweet reaction to the news by the Polish people. Since the Allies recognized the communist government of Poland as an entreaty to the Soviets, Poles abroad were left without a home of a free Poland to return to. Instead, Wesley and his sister would make passage on British ships to Lebanon, where they would live for nearly two years. When subsidies ran out for refugees, Wes and Zosia had the choice to return to Poland under the communists or join their older brother, Jurek, in England. The latter was the only reasonable choice, as millions of Poles were being persuaded to go back to Poland by the communists. Wes surmised that the communist government did not appreciate information flowing outside its realm that would paint its paradise in a bad light.

In 1949, after nearly two years in Great Britain and nine years after their first deportation from Poland, Wes received a letter from his aunt in Chicago, inviting him to the United States. On Thanksgiving Day 1949, he arrived after a long thirty-six-hour train journey from Halifax, Nova Scotia. His ten-year odyssey had drawn to a close. Wes was sent to a private boarding school in Wisconsin. He returned to Chicago and put himself through night school at DePaul University, where he earned a degree in chemistry. After a stint in the army, Wes spent his entire working career at Lever Brothers in Whiting Inc. He died on October 13, 2018.[29]

FIGHTING BEHIND THE IRON CURTAIN: A BULGARIAN NATIVE'S ROLE IN CREATING CHAOS AGAINST COMMUNISM

There was deep suspicion of the Soviet Union and its postwar motives, especially with Soviet troops occupying wide swaths of territory and countries in Central and Eastern Europe. Many ethnic nationalities residing in Illinois, especially the Chicago area, viewed the situation with special alarm with family and friends still residing in those regions. With the Second World War winding down, the American public was simply too tired and weary of war against the Soviet Union.

Direct action thus had to take a new approach, starting in the Truman years. George Kennan, who authored the containment policy, worked throughout early postwar years to develop a covert way of unsettling Soviet-occupied lands ranging from the Baltic states to the Adriatic. The plan would entail recruiting refugees from those countries under Soviet rule to train as a fighting force and disrupt the communist rulers. The Truman Doctrine, alongside the Marshall Plan and containment of communism espoused by Kennan, would become the framework of American foreign policy throughout the Cold War era. As a matter of fact, within the Marshall Plan was a 5 percent funding expenditure that went to such training and arming of guerrilla armies of countrymen for the sole purpose of causing havoc and uprisings behind the Iron Curtain.

One individual with Illinois ties involved in the latter type of direct action was George Georgiev (later Georgieff after moving to the United States). Born in 1930 in the village of Dinevo, Bulgaria, Georgiev grew up during the years of the Second World War, witnessing the Bulgarian communist coup in 1944 that was a precursor to decades of communist rule and Soviet influence. George, along with many other young men of his age, was involved with the opposition movement and refused to join the Communist Party. Because of these actions and beliefs, George was not allowed to attend college. After a friend reported his opposition activities to the local party leaders in April 1950, nineteen-year-old George and another friend left their families and homes to escape Bulgaria and avoid being put in a labor camp, as his cousin and other friends had been. The friends walked for three days to Greece and crossed the border on foot. They were eventually picked up by Greek soldiers, processed as refugees and eventually taken to a refugee camp near Athens.

George had been living in the refugee camp for a few months when representatives from the CIA came to the camp to recruit men to train for espionage work. Although George had been waiting for a transport to emigrate, he decided to stay and assist the CIA, as he hoped it would mean he would be able to return to his homeland of Bulgaria. In January 1951, George and about twenty other young men from the refugee camp were flown to Germany to begin their training at a resort villa in the Alps. They trained for three months, learning Morse code and transmitting messages, as well physical self-defense.

After training, George and the rest of his group were sent back to Greece. They were based there for five years, during which time George crossed and re-crossed the border into Bulgaria to collect information about the Communist Party's activities. Groups of two or three men would cross the border and set up base for a few months. They hid in the mountains and made contact with locals, collecting information that they then coded and sent back to the base in Athens. It was dangerous work; one of George's friends was discovered by the militia and killed at the border.

In 1955, Greece and Bulgaria entered into a treaty, and the CIA was no longer allowed to operate in Greece. As such, the men were relieved of their duties. By this time, one of George's uncles was in Germany, so George was able to immigrate to join him. He lived in Germany for two years, working for the U.S. Army as a guard at military depots until he received his visa and a sponsorship to come to America in 1957. He landed in Richmond, Virginia, and soon joined some friends who had settled in Chicago, Illinois. There he worked as a welder and eventually a tool and die maker. In 1958, he married Ursula Mursewski, who had emigrated from East Germany. They raised two children and lived in northern Illinois until moving to Sparta, Wisconsin, in 2004. George lived there until his death on February 19, 2012.

AS A SUCCESSFUL AND popular general, Dwight Eisenhower ran for the presidential nomination on the idea of rolling back communism peacefully in 1952. With the Korean War in full swing and the hunt for communists at home well underway, the American population backed the former Second World War general for president by a large margin. In 1951, $100 million in military aid was secured to support escapees or those living in Iron Curtain countries. That figure would include efforts to upend communist-ruled people in direct action if needed and necessary.

As Ike's term began in 1953, events would dictate the need to roll back communism in Eastern and Central Europe in an offensive manner. Involvement in Korean War was winding down, and Joseph Stalin's death in 1953 changed the course of Soviet/U.S. relations. It was thought that the Soviets might offer an opening to peace talks after the death of their leader. Further eroding confidence and credibility and lowering morale, Eisenhower stood by while Soviet tanks rolled into Poland and Hungary in 1956, crushing popular uprisings. Those behind the Iron Curtain and immigrants back home supported taking the fight to roll back communism. By 1960, though, ideas of rolling back communism had stopped. Anti-communist conservative warriors such as Joseph McCarthy would be out of power in the mid-1950s. In 1961, the Berlin Wall would be erected, and a new chapter of suffering would take hold behind the Iron Curtain as the Soviet-backed governments would continue bowing to Moscow's needs for decades thereafter.

CHAPTER 8

COLD WAR CHESS

BOBBY FISCHER, AN UNLIKELY COLD WARRIOR

When Bobby Fischer won the World Championship in Reykjavik, Iceland, in 1972 over Boris Spassky, he became the first non-Soviet chess champion since 1937, as a span of ten Soviets had kept the title for a period of forty-five years.[30]

Born in Chicago on March 9, 1943, Bobby Fischer's mother, Regina, a United States citizen born in Missouri, had been under watch by the FBI the prior year due to suspicion that she was a Soviet agent. A decade earlier, Regina and her then-husband, Gerhardt Fischer, a self-described communist, fled to Moscow in 1933 from Germany in fear of Hitler's rise to power. With instability in Europe, Regina came back to the United States in early 1939, yet Gerhardt was denied entry. She was granted a divorce in 1945.

The FBI would watch Regina more carefully for the next twenty-five years. The agency appeared interested in Gerhardt as well, with a number of pieces of circumstantial evidence to prove that both were a threat to U.S. national security. Although Gerhardt was listed as Bobby's father on the birth certificate, Regina admitted at one point that she had not seen Gerhardt since leaving for the United States in 1939. It was suspected that a Hungarian man named Paul Nemenyi, a physicist working in the United States, was his real father. Paul died in 1952 and never met Bobby.

After moving to Brooklyn, Regina bought Bobby his first chess set and spent many hours with him at the Brooklyn Chess Club, where he was coached by the president of the club. In July 1956, Bobby became the youngest to win the United States Junior Chess Championship. In 1957, he became the

Left: Soviet grand master Mikhail Botvinni.

Opposite, left: Bobby Fischer in a high school photo.

Opposite, right: Bobby Fischer prior to a match.

youngest United States champion, just shy of his fifteenth birthday. With an appeal written to Soviet leader Nikita Khrushchev by Regina, Bobby was allowed to visit Moscow in 1958. He was denied proper games of chess with any Soviet grandmaster during his visit, however, and developed an anti-Soviet attitude as a result. He complained incessantly about Soviet collusion between their players and staged his first of many retirements at the ripe age of twenty-one.

Choice words with Fidel Castro would arise in 1965, when Fischer was invited to play a tournament in Cuba. There were severe restrictions on traveling to Cuba, so Fischer arranged to play his chess moves in New York while the games took place in Havana. When Castro tried to make a political statement about Fischer's involvement, Fischer responded that he would withdraw. Castro called his bluff, and Fischer played as expected, earning $10,000 for his "appearance" in the tournament.

When Fischer actually played the game, his constant demands riled organizers and opponents alike. Lamps had to display light in the correct fashion. Cameramen and spectators could be demanded to be replaced or thrown out at a moment's notice. Fischer would leave tournaments in the

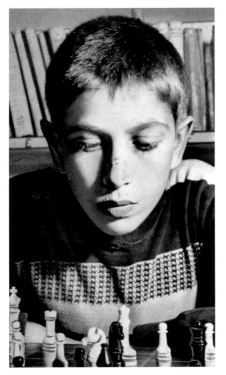

middle of games without warning. Oftentimes he would show up to games with a few minutes on the clock, rattling his opponents, who would object to his behavior.

Prior to his highly anticipated televised match with Boris Spassky in 1972, the two faced each other four times, with the record in favor of Spassky, two draws and two wins. Spassky's background and road to chess was much more drastic than that of Bobby Fischer. Spassky was born in Leningrad in 1937 during the Great Terror, induced by suspicious plots imagined by Stalin. In 1941, the Germans invaded Leningrad from the east, resulting in Spassky's mother fleeing on a train west toward Moscow.

Ideology played a key role in the development of chess in the Soviet Union. Chess was admired by Tsar Nicolas II, but the game was revered during the revolution and thereby branded a "socialist" sport. Chess could be picked up by collective farmer or high-ranking party member, thus being widely available for the entire country to embrace. Mikhail Botvinnik became arguably one of the best chess players in history. The electrical engineer would hold five titles between 1948 and 1963. By the time of Botvinnik's initial run at titles in 1948, Spassky was eleven years old and earning 1,200 rubles per month from the Soviet government, which was more than an engineer earned during that time. Spassky would make it to the top of the chess world as a champion in 1969, the same year Bobby Fischer would make a run at unseating the Soviet champion.

The biggest obstacle early on was adhering to the rules of championship play, which required players to go through Interzonals, Candidates and, finally, to the World Championship tournament. Fischer, as usual, refused to play by the rules in prior years and was able to gain entry into the Interzonals by having Lieutenant Colonel Ed Edmundsen, chairman of the United States Chess Federation, "buy off" two of the American players set to participate in the tournament. Bobby Fischer was a ticket to more viewers, inducing interest in a sport that generally lacked exciting superstars, unlike other American champions in football, baseball, basketball and other sports. Edmundson also promised Fischer the opportunity to earn up to $19,000 in the several stages of the tournaments, along with double the expense money and the best accommodations in hotels along the way.

Before the World Championship match in Iceland, Fischer demanded more prize money. With a benefactor doubling the prize money to $250,000, he finally agreed to play. This would not stop Fischer from skipping out on the opening ceremonies and causing more consternation among all involved (including asking for intercession by Henry Kissinger). Fischer alternated his stays in Reykjavik at a hotel and at the United States Naval Air Station, where he felt more at home and secure from possible interference from the KGB.

A CHAMPION IS CROWNED

After moving from the public arena into the smaller back room to commence the rest of the series, Fischer went on and was finally crowned champion after Spassky conceded. Fischer would eventually win the match with Spassky 12½–8½ and become the eleventh world chess champion. He returned to the United States a hero, have finally beaten the Soviets at their own game and dominance for decades in the sport. Fischer turned down a number of endorsements worth well into the millions of dollars.

In 1975, Bobby Fischer relinquished his world championship title to Anatoly Karpov after not showing for the match. Fischer would become more reclusive, listening to Christian preachers on radio broadcasts and

Gary Kasparov in Dubai.

Boris Spassky.

becoming paranoid that the Soviets were on to him. He went so far as to replace all of his metallic fillings for fear the Soviets beaming malignant waves into his teeth. In 1981, he was mistaken for a bank robber in California and held in jail for two days before being released. He would become a vagabond, turning up in Germany, Hungary and Japan in future years. Fischer and Spassky came back to the chess board in 1992 after prize money of $5 million was placed for the match, to take place in Belgrade, Yugoslavia. Sanctions prohibited Fischer from appearing at the match, but he defied the order anyway. After the 9/11 Islamic militant hijackers attacked United States targets in Washington, D.C., and New York City, Fischer exclaimed, "Well, America got what it deserved." In other bizarre behavior, Fischer was a Holocaust denier. Fischer eventually took up residency in Iceland and became a citizen. Fischer passed away in January 2008 and is buried in Iceland.

CHAPTER 9

PHOTOGRAPHING APOLLO 11

TEENAGERS CAPTURE THE RACE TO THE MOON

In the summer of 1969, David Chudwin confided that he had a choice for his one week of work that summer at a men's clothing store: attend Woodstock in New York or the Apollo 11 Moon launch in Florida. David stated unequivocally that he had chosen wisely. In 1969, while at the University of Michigan, David and his longtime friend Marvin Rubenstein were offered this once-in-a-lifetime opportunity to photograph the Moon launch as one of only three student journalists. They would become the youngest NASA-credentialed journalists in history at the ripe ages of nineteen and eighteen, respectively. By attending the launch, their coverage would allow tens of thousands of college students—through 1,200 college newspapers affiliated through the College Press Service (CPS) Wire Network—to experience stories and photographs of what would become the first landing of humans on the Moon.

At that time, news was dispersed in radio and newspaper format, as the internet was in its infancy, primarily as a nuclear weapons tracking system in the Bay Area of California. The Apollo 11 program would cap off the success of President Kennedy's bold initiative to land a man on the Moon before the decade of the 1960s ended. The space program had different goals and phases. Project Mercury recruited the initial seven men who would become astronauts to experience space orbital missions in the United States. Project Gemini would entail a two-man crew launched into outer space. Project Apollo, the third phase, would land men on the Moon. It was the eleventh mission and would become the apex of such an endeavor, with teenagers David and Marvin witnessing a phenomenal international historical event firsthand.

Apollo 11 crew. *Left to right*: Michael Collins, Buzz Aldrin and Neil Armstrong. *Courtesy of David Chudwin.*

CONTEXT OF THE SPACE RACE

As the Cold War approached its second decade, the external atmosphere of space became an uncharted and challenged battleground between the two superpowers. Superiority of space, designs for human space travel and the prestige of the best system of government were at stake. More importantly to both sides of the Cold War were any military weaponry, communications systems and surveillance that could gain them an upper edge in a potential conflict of a third world war. Enter Sputnik, the first man-made satellite built by the Soviet Union; it became a scientific and military symbol that would change history and send mankind vaulting into the void of space.

Sputnik, meaning "satellite" in Russian, was in sporting parlance a game changer, dealing a significant blow to the United States in the race to space. At the time of its launch in 1957, most Americans held a sense of confidence that the technological capabilities of their country were second to none. After all, America, with its newfound peacetime abundance and booming economy, was on the cutting edge and leading the world in innovations, spanning everything from transistor radios to a cure for polio. But when the Soviet Union launched Sputnik into space, it catapulted itself into the lead of the Space Race. The stakes had been incomparably raised in the Cold War. Americans were fearful of sleeping at night under a "communist moon."

THE PIVOTAL MOMENT OF SPUTNIK

Nikita Khrushchev's gamble on space paid off when history was made on October 4, 1957. After several years in development, Sputnik was planned in accordance with the International Geophysical Year (IGY) from July 1, 1957, to December 31, 1958. This period was designed to foster more cooperation in the world's efforts to understand the sciences. Both the United States and Soviet Union pledged to launch satellites during the IGY. Not to be outdone, each side would use the occasion not only as a diplomatic show of goodwill but also to test its military capabilities.

Needless to say, the Sputnik launch ushered in a new era of scientific discovery, wonder and amazement but also a heretofore unforeseen fear of Cold War consequences. Sputnik's presence in space caused alarm all over the United States and fostered a new approach to federalizing education, highlighting the need for science, math and engineering in American school systems. After all, superiority in conquering the heavens had a direct implication on intercontinental ballistic missiles carrying nuclear payloads to opposing forces of any country. The Sputnik satellite, although crude in design compared to technology today, covered nearly every habitable place on Earth over the skies above during its orbit. There was no place to hide from the reach of the Soviets' technological and military edge. It was therefore necessary for the United States to put immediate resources into finding a way to get the upper hand in the Space Race. One significant reaction in the United States was the creation of the National Aeronautics and Space Act in 1958, which resulted in the creation of the National Aeronautics and Space Administration (NASA).

The U.S. Department of Defense watched with unease and concern, immediately responding to the ensuing political furor by approving funding for another U.S. satellite project to compete with the Vanguard satellite program. As a simultaneous alternative to Vanguard, Wernher von Braun and his Army Redstone Arsenal team began work on the Explorer project. Explorer I would launch successfully in January 1958. This launch allowed the United States to keep up in the Space Race and save face by launching a satellite as promised during the International Geophysical Year.

For its part, the United States had been working on the Vanguard satellite program for years. The Vanguard weighed in considerably lighter than its Soviet counterpart at 3.5 pounds. After taking second place in a two-man race to space, with Sputnik entering the heavens first, insult led to injury as the Vanguard launch on December 6, 1957, was a complete disaster. The rocket fell back to the launch pad a mere two seconds after liftoff. The small Vanguard satellite flew off and was too damaged to recover or reuse. A black eye to the United States space program was met with glee by the Soviet Union in the Space Race. Some labeled the United States effort "Flopnik" and "Kaputnik." The naval Vanguard program would be scrapped, and Wernher von Braun would lead his scientific and engineering team of American and former German colleagues in the Explorer satellite program, which would launch in January 1958 to stymie momentum held by the Soviet space achievements.

Meanwhile, as the United States satellite efforts fell flat, the Soviets continued to march along their path to cementing space superiority. Sputnik II was launched barely one month after the initial Sputnik on November 3, 1957. As with the United States' space goals, the Sputnik series of launches was built on the premise of sending humans into outer space. This particular Sputnik launch was memorable in that it involved a dog named Laika. Laika would become the first dog and animal to orbit Earth. She had been preceded in the animal sequence of space visitors by fruit flies, mice, American monkeys and other Soviet dogs, all launched on prior missions to just above the atmosphere by both the Soviet Union and the United States. Within a few years of Laika's historical space visit, frogs and rabbits would also soon hitch rides into outer space. Sadly, the Soviets did not place an emphasis on having animals return safely, and Laika died of heat exhaustion after five hours in space. The Soviet Sputnik II mission helped achieve a scientific first when the first human to orbit the earth was launched from an advanced Vostok rocket one year later. Yuri Gagarin, Soviet cosmonaut, represented humanity's first orbital passenger on April 12, 1961. It further cemented the Soviet position as leading the charge into space.

With the American space program underway, setbacks occurred, such as the Apollo 1 mission that ended in tragedy during a simulation mission. During a prelaunch test in January 1967, astronauts Gus Grissom, Roger B. Chaffee and Ed White died of asphyxiation in the command module after it caught fire. The astronauts could not escape and perished immediately. Each and every one of these space events was chronicled and followed tenaciously by David Chudwin and Marvin Rubenstein while growing up in Chicago.

GROWING UP COLD WAR

David's father was a U.S. Army medic stationed in Germany from 1947 to 1949. After spending six weeks in Vienna, the couple wanted to take in a musical in the Soviet-occupied zone of that city. Vienna, similar to Berlin, was occupied in quadrants by the French, British, Americans and Soviets. David's father was told by a general that the Soviet zone was not a safe place for Americans, let alone servicemen and doctors. The latter were subject to kidnapping, in an effort to coax their talents for use in the communist zone due to a shortage of medical professionals and quality medical care.[31]

Born shortly after David's father returned from his U.S. Army time in West Germany in 1950, David would become enthralled with the Space Race at the young age of seven. The Sputnik launch by the Soviets in 1957 changed the adversarial military dynamic between the USSR and the United States. The dominance of space, which began with a series of "beeps" transmitted from orbit to the ground, would be of extreme importance for both nations' survival. With his earliest memories shaped by the Cold War events of 1956, the Hungarian Uprising of that year captured young David's attention. His attention to the era was punctuated by fear of atomic war, as the Soviets had tested their atomic bomb and subsequently a hydrogen bomb that could be deployed by long-range Soviet bombers. The "duck and cover" drill was perfected by David and millions of others, taking refuge under desks at school, tables or even picnic blankets (as demonstrated by civil defense films featuring Burt the Turtle). As David grew older, his interest in space expanded as developments furthered the race into the final frontier. He read every book, magazine and pamphlet on the subject. It would be fair to say that every success and setback in the space program were met emotionally, just as the astronauts and those who worked in the space program felt. The 1960s would become more intertwined with the Cold War era as David's journey captured the essence of the Space Race with the Apollo 11 launch in 1969.

JFK's declaration to land a man on the Moon by the end of the decade was a clarion call to catch up and surpass that Soviets in space. A key development occurred during the Bay of Pigs invasion in 1961, when the United States was occupied with overthrowing the Castro regime in that

Lyndon Johnson, General William Westmoreland and other dignitaries observe the Apollo 11 launch. *Courtesy of David Chudwin.*

country. JFK wrote a memo to Vice President Lyndon Johnson asking him to issue a directive. LBJ was appointed the head of the president's Space Council and steered much of the space program operations to Houston, Texas, which was Johnson's home state. Johnson had served in the U.S. House of Representatives and the U.S. Senate.

David's choice of college came down to a few locations: the University of Wisconsin–Madison, where his father and mother had met, and the University of Michigan–Ann Arbor. As a matter of fact, his choice really hinged on which campus offered a less militant, antiwar environment. He chose to attend college in Ann Arbor, just as the University of Wisconsin campus was to become more tumultuous, with Dow Chemical protests and the New Year's Gang bombings in 1969–70, among other headline protests. However, the University of Michigan was not spared by any means. As a school journalist there, David was the subject of a file at the FBI as a person of interest, not unlike many students on campus who were being watched both by informants and by local police. David recalled finding himself covering a protest on campus involving the trial of the Chicago Seven and SDS persons, including Bernardine Dohrn. Despite his press badge David was followed into an alley while leaving, as students had started throwing rocks at the police. The policeman had his gun drawn on David while following him into the alley.

With an interest in politics, David was an active member of Eugene McCarthy's bid to become the Democratic nominee for the 1968 presidential race. He went so far as to host a fundraiser for the Minnesota senator at his home in Chicago, where one hundred people attended. As he left home to go back to the University of Michigan for school during the 1968 Democratic Convention in Chicago, volunteers from the McCarthy campaign were beaten and arrested during violent episodes during the convention.

His recollection of Apollo 8 on December 24, 1968, was seeing the crew flying near the surface of the Moon. Grainy footage of Bill Anders, Jim Lovell and Frank Borman was accompanied by a Christmas Eve message that included reciting Bible passages to those tuning in from Earth. It was the most watched televised event up to that time in history. It brought tears to his eyes while listening in.

David was equally thrilled covering the hometown natives Jim McDivvot and Ed White during a visit to Chicago in June 1967. Ed White was the first human to walk in space. White's life would end prematurely and tragically in a training simulation on the ground during testing of Apollo 1. White,

Gus Grissom and Roger Chafee would perish when a fire broke out inside their capsule. Crews worked frantically to save the astronauts but were too late. The bodies of each of them were motionless as they asphyxiated within minutes in an environment of 100 percent oxygen.

APOLLO 11

There was no telling if Apollo 11 was certain to be *the* Moon landing mission, as the nation (including David and Marvin) held its collective breath that Apollo 9 and 10 would be successful. Since the Apollo 11 mission had a window of launch on July 16, David and Marvin planned their travel accordingly, giving themselves a cushion of a few days on either side of that date. Coincidentally, Marvin usually stayed with family in upstate New York each summer. That summer of 1969, his family invited him to a then unknown festival called Woodstock. Marvin declined. Like David, Marvin considered the Apollo excitement to be superior to a music festival—barely anyone at the time would have guessed its attendance and significance.

The two young journalists arrived on July 13 in Cape Canaveral, looking forward to taking part in private tours and getting as close to the launch pad as any human possibly could prior to launch (approximately two thousand feet, according to Marvin). NASA buses were reserved and used throughout the week; the transportation options for attending an event that was expected to draw 1 million visitors caused major congestion in an underdeveloped region. Since there were no internet reservations for cars, airfare and motels at that time, David fondly recalled out the belabored process. He was quick to point out that motel reservations, for example, were confirmed with a postcard by mail. The motel on Cocoa Beach, appropriately called the Sea Missile Motel, ran ten dollars per night for six nights.

Upon arrival at the Melbourne airport, the two were introduced to four astronauts who were at the airport to pick up their wives: Jim Irwin (Apollo 15), Alan Bean (Apollo 12), Charles Duke (who would land on the Moon on Apollo 16) and Bruce McCandless (shuttle pilot and first astronaut to attempt a tether-less spacewalk). VIP tours of the NASA complex included viewing the launch pads and space preparations of Mercury, Gemini and Apollo astronauts. An engineer stated the grim fact that 4.7 million pounds of compressed fuel were present for the launch. If it were to explode, it would be comparable to the Hiroshima blast. Since the viewing area was a mere three miles away, this solemn fact caught the boys' attention. When liftoff occurred, the heat from the engines could still be felt at such a distance.[32]

As the week progressed, David and Marvin attended and covered briefings with panels that included Wernher von Braun and Walter Cronkite. The crew of Apollo 11—Neil Armstrong, Buzz Aldrin and Michael Collins—was in quarantine so as to not fall ill during the mission. The astronauts, however, were able to link via televised interview on July 14, two days before the launch.

When launch day arrived, the weather was perfect. David and Marvin hopped on the transport to position themselves for the astronauts' walk off the ramp and onto their transport to take them to the launch pad. Unbeknownst to David, he got the photo of a lifetime: a perfect shot of Colling, Armstrong and Aldrin in full space suits coming out of the doors. Nonetheless, it would be several weeks of photo development time before he would know it.

The boys took their places in the seating area reserved for the press to witness the launch going off smoothly. They were surrounded by former president Lyndon Johnson, Vice President Spiro Agnew, General William Westmoreland and such luminaries as Johnny Carson, Ed McMahon and actor Hugh O' Brien. On the way out of the viewing area, David and Marvin bumped into astronaut Fred Haise, who would be on the ill-fated Apollo 13 mission that thankfully made it back to Earth. The Apollo 13 mission popularized the phrase "Houston, we've had a problem here." Apollo 11's successful mission, in the meantime, was an accomplishment for mankind and the U.S. space program. The Soviets attempted to upstage the mission by sending their own rock collecting mission to the Moon during that week but aborted. The Americans won the race to the Moon, an accomplishment that excited the nation and brought it together during the depths of a contentious era that witnessed Vietnam War and civil rights protests.

LIST OF ASTRONAUTS IN THE UNITED STATES SPACE PROGRAM FROM ILLINOIS

CERNAN, Eugene A., Captain, U.S. Navy (Retired)
The eleventh man to walk on the Moon
Born on March 14, 1934, in Chicago, Illinois
Bachelor of Science in electrical engineering from Purdue University; Master of Science in aeronautical engineering from U.S. Navy Postgraduate School

Flew on Gemini IX, Apollo 10 and Apollo 17
Cumulative hours of spaceflight: more than 566
Cumulative EVA time: more than 73 hours

MATTINGLY, Thomas K., II, Rear Admiral, U.S. Navy
Born on March 17, 1936, in Chicago, Illinois
Bachelor of Science in aeronautical engineering from Auburn University
Flew on Apollo 16, STS-4 and STS 51-C
Cumulative hours of spaceflight: more than 508
Cumulative EVA time: more than 1 hour

McDIVITT, James A., Brigadier General, U.S. Air Force (Retired)
Born on June 10, 1929, in Chicago, Illinois
Bachelor of Science in aeronautical engineering from University of Michigan
Flew on Gemini IV and Apollo 9 and was the Apollo Spacecraft program manager
Cumulative hours of spaceflight: more than 338

CHAPTER 10

THE AGE OF WALT DISNEY

Walt Disney was born on December 5, 1901, in Chicago, and after his family spent more than a decade living in Missouri, the Disney family moved back to Chicago. At an early age, Walt was enamored of drawing and cartooning. After returning to the Chicago, he took art classes at the Chicago Academy of Fine Arts. He earned money in part by being a substitute mail carrier. In September 1918, Walt Disney was in the Chicago Federal Building during a bombing campaign, supposedly in retaliation for the Industrial Workers of the World Trial that had been taken place in the days prior.

Wernher von Braun, then chief of Guided Missile Development Operation Division at Army Ballistic Missile Agency (ABMA) at Redstone Arsenal, Alabama, was visited by Walt Disney in 1954. In the 1950s, von Braun worked with Disney Studio as a technical director, making three films about space exploration for television.[33]

Von Braun would serve as technical advisor on three space-related television films that Disney produced in the 1950s. Together, von Braun (the engineer) and Disney (the artist) used the new medium of television to illustrate how high man might fly on the strength of technology and the spirit of human imagination. According to David R. Smith, director of archives at Walt Disney Productions, von Braun caught the attention of Disney senior producer Ward Kimball. The *Collier's* series had appeared about the time noting that Disney decided to use television to promote Disneyland in California. The theme park would include four major sections:

Wernher Von Braun.

Fantasyland, Frontierland, Adventureland and Tomorrowland. Disney producers would incorporate ideas from Disney fantasy films like *Snow White*, *Pinocchio* and others to promote the first area of the park. The second and third areas would be built around Davy Crockett and other adventure films. Tomorrowland, however, represented a real challenge. In response, Kimball contacted von Braun, who, according to Smith, "pounced on the

Walt Disney with Wernher Von Braun.

opportunity." As a technical consultant for Disney, von Braun would join Heinz Haber, a specialist in the emerging field of space and medicine, and Willy Ley, a famous rocket historian. All three space experts had coauthored the *Collier's* series. Disney personally introduced the first television show, *Man in Space*, which aired on ABC on March 9, 1955. The objective, he said, was to combine "the tools of our trade with the knowledge of the scientists to give a factual picture of the latest plans for man's newest adventure." He later called the show "science factual." The show represented something new in its approach to science. But it also relied on Disney's trademark animation techniques.[34]

WARTIME AND COLD WAR FILMS

With Disneyland's beginnings during the Second World War, Walt Disney also commissioned a 1958 episode of Disneyland's *Magic Highway USA*, which covered the broad evolution and history of American motoring. But it was the last nine minutes, an animated segment called "The Road Ahead," where Disney's Imagineers were let loose, creating "a realistic look at the road ahead and what tomorrow's motorist can expect in the years to come."

At the time, President Eisenhower was advocating for stronger transport links across the United States, especially to move troops and supplies in the event of an attack, a tangible fear in the developing Cold War. In 1956, he signed the Federal Aid Highway Act into law: forty-one thousand miles of new roads would be built, the largest public works project in American history at that point. Partly funded by the Portland Cement Association, *Magic Highway USA* was Disney's attempt to try to shape the vision of these future roads.[35]

In 1947, Walt Disney would cofound the Motion Picture Alliance for the Preservation of American Ideals (MPA), a political action group. The group would go so far as to issue a pamphlet advising producers on the avoidance of "subtle communistic touches" in their films. Its counsel revolved around a list of ideological prohibitions, such as "Don't smear the free-enterprise system....Don't smear industrialists....Don't smear wealth....Don't smear the profit motive....Don't deify the 'common man'....Don't glorify the collective."

CHAPTER 11

ASSASSINATING CASTRO

CHICAGO MAFIA GETS THE CALL

Fidel Castro's revolutionary career began while he was enrolled at the School of Law of the University of Havana, when he participated in resistance movements in the Dominican Republic and Colombia. He became active in Cuban politics after graduating in 1950, and he prepared to run for legislative office in the 1952 elections. Those elections were canceled when Fulgencio Batista forcibly seized power. Castro began organizing a resistance movement against Cuba's new dictator, leading several ill-fated attempts against Batista's forces, such as the assault on Santiago de Cuba and another on Cuba's eastern coast. The tide of battle would turn, however. Castro's guerrilla warfare campaign and his propaganda efforts succeeded in eroding the power of Batista's military and popular support while also attracting volunteers to the revolutionary cause. Batista was forced to flee the country in 1959. Shortly after, Castro assumed complete authority over Cuba's new government.

In 1959, during the ouster, the U.S. Navy was off the coast in the form of the USS *Kitty Hawk*. On the *Kitty Hawk* was the author's uncle Jim Sturdevant, who resided in Loves Park, Illinois for many years. Jim was a short-order cook during his service time in the navy and reminisced occasionally about the mission undertaken against the Batista regime. The United States military orders dictated blockading and shutting off supplies to Cuba, which included shutting off the water to Batista and his cronies. Batista would abdicate his power and flee to Miami, where he would live out his final days with expatriates of Cuba.

Left: Che Guevara with Fidel Castro. *Right*: Cuban leader Fidel Castro.

It is widely reputed and was partially corroborated by the Church Committee hearings that during the Kennedy administration, the Central Intelligence Agency (CIA) recruited Sam Giancana and other mobsters to assassinate Fidel Castro. Giancana reportedly said that CIA and the Cosa Nostra were "different sides of the same coin." Documents released in 2017 showed the Giancana connection to CIA and to Robert Maheu.

Judith Exner claimed to be the mistress of both Giancana and JFK and that she delivered communications between them about Castro. Giancana's daughter Antoinette has stated that her father was performing a scam to pocket millions of CIA dollars.[36]

Documents released during 1997 revealed that some Mafiosi worked with CIA on assassination attempts against Castro. CIA documents released during 2007 confirmed that during the summer of 1960, the CIA recruited ex-FBI agent Maheu to meet with the West Coast representative of the Chicago mob, Johnny Roselli. When Maheu contacted Roselli, Maheu hid that he was sent by the CIA, instead portraying himself an advocate for international corporations. He offered $150,000 to have Castro killed, but Roselli refused any pay. Roselli introduced Maheu to two men he called Sam Gold (Giancana) and Joe. "Joe" was Santo Trafficante Jr., the Tampa/Miami syndicate boss and one of the most powerful mobsters in pre-revolution

Cuba. Glenn Kessler of the *Washington Post* explained: "After Fidel Castro led a revolution that toppled the government of Fulgencio Batista in 1959, CIA was desperate to eliminate Castro. So, the agency sought out a partner equally worried about Castro—the Mafia, which had lucrative investments in Cuban casinos."

According to the declassified CIA "Family Jewels" documents, Giancana and Trafficante were contacted in September 1960 about the possibility of an assassination attempt by Maheu after Maheu had contacted Roselli, a Mafia member in Las Vegas and Giancana's number-two man. Maheu had presented himself as a representative of numerous international businesses in Cuba that Castro was expropriating. He offered $150,000 for the "removal" of Castro through this operation (the documents suggest that neither Roselli nor Giancana nor Trafficante accepted any payment for the job). Giancana suggested using poison pills to dose Castro's food and drink. The CIA gave these pills to Giancana's nominee, Juan Orta, whom Giancana presented

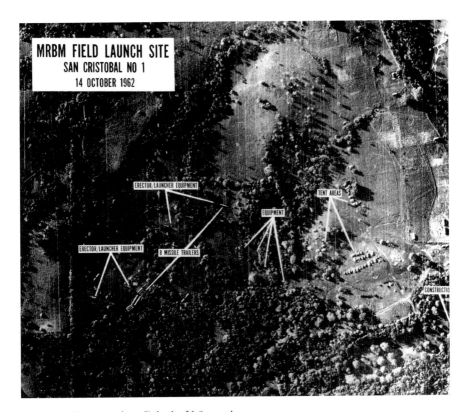

Soviet missiles spotted on Cuba by U-2 spy plane.

as a corrupt official in the new Cuban government and who had access to Castro. After six attempts to introduce the poison into Castro's food, Orta abruptly demanded to be relieved from the mission, giving the job to another, unnamed participant. Later, Giancana and Trafficante made a second attempt using Anthony Verona, the commander of the Cuban Exile Junta who had, according to Trafficante, become "disaffected with the apparent ineffectual progress of the Junta." Verona requested $10,000 in expenses and $1,000 worth of communications equipment. How much work was performed for the second attempt is unknown, as the entire program was canceled soon thereafter due to the Bay of Pigs invasion in April 1961. The following year, the Cuban Missile Crisis would become yet another obstacle, this time with nuclear missiles being placed in Cuba by the Soviets. Nuclear war was barely averted, with missiles sent back by barge to the Soviet Union when Nikita Khrushchev blinked on the verge of disaster.

According to the "Family Jewels," Giancana asked Maheu to wire the room of his then mistress, Phyllis McGuire, whom he suspected of having an affair with comedian Dan Rowan. Although documents suggest that Maheu acquiesced, the device was not planted due to the arrest of the agent who had been tasked with planting it. According to the documents, Robert F. Kennedy prohibited the prosecution of the agent and of Maheu, who was soon linked to the wire attempt, at the CIA's request. Giancana and McGuire, who had a long-lasting affair, were originally introduced by Frank Sinatra. According to Antoinette Giancana, during part of the affair, McGuire had a concurrent affair with President Kennedy.[37]

CHAPTER 12

LIST OF MILITARY BASES IN ILLINOIS DURING THE COLD WAR

The only U.S. Air Force base named after an enlisted airman, Scott Air Force Base has undergone many different missions and provided many functions during its existence since its inception in 1917. The air force became a separate service in 1947, and Scott Field officially became Scott Air Force Base on January 13, 1948. Scott's communications training mission continued into the 1950s, and the base's aeromedical mission continued to grow. By the end of 1950, Douglas C-54 Skymasters were bringing two hundred patients per week to Scott from Korea. In August 1957, many of Scott's radio courses moved to Lackland Air Force Base, Texas, and by 1959, the remaining courses were either phased out or moved to other bases.

In October 1957, responsibility for Scott moved from Air Training Command (ATC) to Military Air Transport Service (MATS). As a consequence of the realignment, Scott's wing host, the 3,310th Technical Training Wing, was re-designated on October 1, 1957, as the 1,405th Air Base Wing. In the years following the transition, Scott's central location and extensive medical facilities led to it becoming an aeromedical evacuation hub. On June 1, 1964, the 1,405th was re-designated as the 1,405th Aeromedical Transport Wing in conjunction with its assuming responsibility for all aeromedical evacuation operations within the continental United States. However, the 1,405th would only fill this role for about eighteen months due to a major airlift reorganization.

As part of an air force consolidation of strategic, tactical and logistics airlift under one command, MATS was re-designated as Military Airlift

Command (MAC) on January 1, 1966. In support of the reorganization, the 375th Troop Carrier Wing was re-designated in December 1965 as the 375th Aeromedical Airlift Wing (AAW) and was subsequently activated and organized on Scott AFB on January 12, 1966. In accordance with the activation order, the 375th assumed all the resources and manpower of the 1,405[th] as that wing was discontinued. The addition of a fleet of C9A Nightingales in 1968 further expanded the 375th's aeromedical mission, and by 1970, the 375th AAW was moving an average of 60,600 patients per year, mainly from the Vietnam theater.

In 1973, the Paris Peace Accords were signed, ending the United States' involvement in the Vietnam War. That same year, the 375th AAW's Patient Airlift center coordinated sixty-one aeromedical missions to bring 367 former POWs back to the U.S. in Operation Homecoming.

By 1978, the 375th had taken on the mission of Operational Support Airlift and was managing a dispersed continental fleet of T-39A Saberliners, which flew a combined ninety-two thousand hours per year, flying passengers and cargo around the world. The T-39As were eventually phased out in 1984, and Scott received C-21A Learjets.[38]

GREAT LAKES NAVAL STATION

Opened in 1911, Naval Station Great Lakes (NSGL) is the navy's largest training installation and the home of the navy's only boot camp. Located on more than 1,600 acres overlooking Lake Michigan, the installation includes 1,153 buildings, with 39 in the National Register of Historic Places. NSGL supports more than fifty tenant commands and elements, as well as more than twenty thousand sailors, Marines, soldiers and DoD civilians who live and work on the installation.[39]

CHANUTE-RANTOUL AFB

Chanute Air Force Base (AFB) was an air force training facility located in the east-central Illinois village of Rantoul. On May 23, 1917, the United States government signed a contract leasing 640 acres of agricultural land in Rantoul, Illinois, for a new aviation field to train World War I pilots. With the end of the war on November 11, 1918, the base's function changed from a pilot training facility to a storage depot for aircraft engines, paint and other miscellaneous surplus items. Between 1921 and 1926, Chanute Field experienced a resurgence in activity, and in 1939, an additional 276 acres west of the airfield and east of Route 45 were acquired. Following construction in the late 1930s and early 1940s, Chanute Field became a state-of-the-art facility, well prepared to train ground crews for World War II. In the early 1950s, training was offered to military personnel at Chanute AFB to include intercontinental ballistic missile (ICBM) training. A ballistic missile training building was constructed in 1959. Military flight operations were terminated in July 1971, at which time it became a non-flying training base. All military operations ceased in September 1993 as Chanute AFB was selected for closured during Base Realignment and Closure (BRAC) in 1988.[40]

JOLIET ARMY AMMUNITION ARSENAL

The Joliet Army Ammunition Plant (JOAAP) was originally known as the Elwood Ordnance Plant (EOP) and the Kankakee Ordnance Works (KOW) when they were authorized by the federal government in 1940. The federal government purchased 36,645 acres from local farmers at a cost of $8,175,815. Construction costs totaled more than $81 million. Seventy-seven such plants were built during World War II to produce ammunition and explosives for the U.S. military. At the time they were built, the Joliet plants were considered the largest, most sophisticated munitions plants in the world. Both the Elwood and Kankakee plants became a training base that supported the Allies' efforts. At peak production during the Second World War, more than 10,425 people were employed at the two plants. The Elwood facility loaded more than 926 million bombs, shells, mines, detonators, fuzes and boosters, and the Kankakee facility set a national record producing more than 1 billion pounds of TNT.

The Elwood and Kankakee Plants were combined and re-designated the Joliet Arsenal in 1945, when operations were placed on standby. The arsenal was reactivated in 1952–57 during the Korean War and again during the Vietnam War. TNT production stopped in 1976, and by the late 1970s, most operations had ceased. The total size of the Joliet Army Ammunition Plant at the time it was declared inactive in 1993 was 23,543 acres, according to information provided by the USDA Department of Forestry.[41]

RECLAMATION OF LAND

To date, 15,080 acres have been transferred to the U.S. Forest Service for the establishment of the Midewin National Tallgrass Prairie, 2,243 acres to the State of Illinois for subsequent transfer to CenterPoint Properties, 982 acres for the Abraham Lincoln National Cemetery and 455 acres to Will County to establish a landfill.

Other transfers include nearly 10 acres to the U.S. Forest Service for a maintenance facility and 218 acres to the Joliet Arsenal Development Authority. The remaining 761 acres are planned for transfer to the Joliet Arsenal Development Authority in 2011, according to information courtesy the U.S. Army Corps of Engineers/Louisville District.

THE ROCK ISLAND ARMY ARSENAL

The Rock Island area was first used for military purposes in 1816 with the construction of Fort Armstrong. The fort was part of a system of defenses in the Upper Mississippi Valley and served as a mustering point and headquarters during the Black Hawk War of 1832. The fort was abandoned in 1836, but it remained in use as an ordnance depot until 1845.

The military facility of Rock Island Arsenal was established by an act of Congress. In 1862, it turned over to the command of the Department of the Army. During the Civil War, the Rock Island Arsenal was used as a Union prison camp, and the Rock Island Prison Barracks were constructed in December 1863. The prison facility was used until July 1865 as part of a twenty-one-camp system used by Union forces. At its height, 12,192 Confederate prisoners were held at the Rock Island Prison Barracks, where 1,964 of them died. The only visible remains of the Rock Island Prison Barracks today is the Confederate Cemetery, where all 1,964 casualties of the prison were buried. A separate cemetery, the Rock Island National Cemetery, was established in 1863 as site to bury Union prison staff who died on the island, 125 in all. Today, it is one of 117 national cemeteries controlled and operated by the U.S. Veterans Administration.

In 1880, the Rock Island Arsenal was used for the manufacture of government weapons, supplies and ordnance. On July 4, 1905, the Rock Island Arsenal Museum was established and is now the second-oldest army museum after West Point. Exhibits at the museum detail the island's history as a Union prison camp during the Civil War and provide examples of weapons and ordnance produced throughout its history.

In 1919, the base began producing Liberty Mark VIII tanks, the first generation of American tanks, stopping production in 1920. Following the First World War, the Rock Island Arsenal took on the role of producing weapons, vehicles and ordnance for the army. This continued during the Second World War and well into the Cold War era, where research and development procured and produced howitzers and rockets (Little John and Honest John), as well as atomic cannons. It produced 53 of the cannons during the Cold War until shutting down production in 1961.

Today, the Rock Island Arsenal hosts the second-largest U.S. Army museum and showcases war materiel from all eras, including the post–Second World War era in the fight against communism around the globe during the Cold War. An experimental model of the M65 atomic cannon, adopted in 1956, could fire both nuclear and conventional shells up to eighteen miles. This mobile cannon weighed in at forty-seven tons, with a prime mover consisting of both a front and rear truck that could reach speeds of thirty miles per hour. The atomic cannon had been replaced by more mobile modern rockets by the mid-1960s.

Howitzers, such as the M115 displayed at the Rock Island Arsenal, were standard issue during wars on the Korean peninsula and Vietnam and serviced by a crew of fourteen. They fired both high-explosive and nuclear shells. Toward the end of the Cold War, this particular howitzer was overhauled at the Rock Island Arsenal and sold to Iran, as that country was allied with the United States until the overthrow of Shah Pahlavi in 1979 by the mullahs and Ayatollah Khomeini. Iraqi troops captured it during the Iran-Iraq War and subsequently captured by U.S. forces during the Gulf War and returned in 1991.

ROCKETS

As the Cold War became a reality after World War II, rocketry took off, with the continued research of the V-2 rockets that Nazi Germany had perfected under the tutelage of Wernher Von Braun and other scientists of the Third Reich. Notably, at the Rock Island Army Arsenal was development of the Honest John Rocket System. The U.S. Army's primary field artillery rocket until the mid-1970s, the rocket carried a nuclear or high-explosive warhead. The rocket was loaded as a truck-mounted, rail-type launcher. In 1955, the USA XM80 Little John rocket was studied in the Research and Development Division to design a towed helicopter-transportable launcher for the 318mm rocket. The Little John Rocket System had three component parts: the rocket, the rocket launcher and the rocket trailer.[42]

CHAPTER 13

COLD WAR CASUALTIES

Long thought of as a war without direct conflict between the Soviet Union and the United States, the Cold War was nonetheless a deadly war with the consequence of loss of human life. As mentioned in the preface, an Allied Expeditionary Force landed inside Bolshevik territory in North Russia and Siberia at the end of the First World War. Direct engagement resulted in casualties, as Americans fought and died inside Russia during its civil war in 1919–20. As Cold War tensions took hold after the Second World War, retrofitted bombers engaged behind enemy territory in "ferret flights" (reconnaissance missions) over Warsaw Pact countries and Soviet republics to test radar capabilities. Some missions would never return, with 126 airmen continuing to be unaccounted for as of this writing. The skies alone would not bear the loss of American service men and women, as the seas would claim lives of American personnel as well. The famous cases of the USS *Thresher* in 1963 and the USS *Scorpion* in 1968 attest to the dangers that lurked for the U.S. Navy while chasing "Ivan" in the oceans around the globe.

THE BERLIN AIRLIFT

The first major confrontation of the Cold War era, after the Allied victories over Nazi Germany, involved the status of Germany and Berlin. According to the treaty at the Yalta Conference, both Germany and the city of Berlin would be divided into four separate zones—controlled by the Americans, the British, the French and the Soviets. Germany was divided into East Germany (German Democratic Republic), controlled by the Soviets, and West Germany (Federal Republic of Germany), controlled by the Western powers. The Americans, British and French decided to consolidate their occupational zones.

The city of Berlin, deep inside East Germany, immediately became a Cold War flashpoint. This would be true of the Cold War era more generally. In June 1948, Joseph Stalin sought to push the West out of Berlin and weaken its resolve in supporting the peoples of West Berlin, cutting off previously agreed-on routes of transit for the Western powers to travel uninhibited through East German territory to reach the beleaguered city.

Instead of directly confronting the Soviets, President Harry Truman authorized an airlift to send vital supplies to West Berlin. These supplies followed air routes that would provide a modicum of safety to drop food, clothing, fuel and other essentials to West Berliners. This process would continue into the fall of 1949, when Stalin backed down and restored ground routes to the city. This confrontation would not be resolved without loss of lives, as First Lieutenant Eugene S. Erickson of Collinsville, Illinois, could attest. According to historian Richard Reeves, Lieutenant Erickson was one of three victims of the first C-54 Skymaster that crashed into the Taunus Mountains on October 18, 1948, just three miles from Rhein-Main.[43]

Following is complete listing of thirty-one American servicemen who died during the Berlin Airlift:

- First Lieutenant George B. Smith, Tuscaloosa, Alabama
- First Lieutenant Leland V. Williams, Abilene, Texas
- Mr. Karl V. Hagen, New York, New York
- First Lieutenant Charles H. King, Britton, South Dakota
- First Lieutenant Robert W. Stuber, Arlington, California
- Major Edwin C. Diltz, Fayetteville, Texas
- Captain Willian R. Howard, Gunnison, Mississippi
- Captain Joel M. deVolentine, Miami, Florida
- First Lieutenant William T. Lucas, Wilson, North Carolina
- Private First Class Johnny T. Orms, Rhein-Main Air Base
- Captain James A. Vaughan, New Haven, Connecticut
- First Lieutenant Eugene S. Erickson, Collinsville, Illinois
- Sergeant Richard Winter, Seattle, Washington

- Captain Billy E. Phelps, Long Beach, California
- First Lieutenant Willis F. Hargis, Nacogdoches, Texas
- Technical Sergeant Lloyd C. Wells, San Antonio, Texas
- Aviation Machinist's Mate Petty Officer Third Class Harry R. Crites Jr., Lafayette, Indiana
- First Lieutenant Richard M. Wurgel, Union City, New Jersey
- First Lieutenant Lowell A. Wheaton Jr., Corpus Christi, Texas
- Captain William A. Rathgeber, Portland, Oregon
- Sergeant Bernard J. Watkins, Lafayette, Indiana
- Corporal Norbert H. Theis, Cunningham, Kansas
- Private First Class Ronald E. Stone, Mount Sterling, Kentucky
- First Lieutenant Ralph H. Boyd, Fort Worth, Texas
- First Lieutenant Craig B. Ladd, Minneapolis, Minnesota
- Technical Sergeant Charles L. Putnam, Colorado Springs, Colorado
- First Lieutenant Robert P. Weaver, Fort Wayne, Indiana
- First Lieutenant Royce C. Stephens, San Antonio, Texas
- First Lieutenant Robert C. von Luehrte, Covington, Kentucky
- Second Lieutenant Donald J. Leemon, Green Bay, Wisconsin
- Technical Sergeant Herbert F. Heinig, Fort Wayne, Indiana

Training accidents were another source of Cold War casualties. On the domestic front, a training accident over Inver Grove Heights resulted in the deaths of seven airmen as a B-52 crashed into a farm field in September 1958. Among the casualties listed was Technical Sergeant Leon R. Lew, a tail gunner from Skokie, Illinois. As the event goes, it was a warm, dark September evening in 1958 when August Kahl and his fifteen-year-old son, Loren, were loading tomatoes onto their farm truck. As a fireball suddenly enveloped the farm, there was little time to make sense of the tragedy unfolding. Only scant minutes before, an Air Force B-52D Stratofortress had been maneuvering at 36,400 feet overhead. On a Cold War training mission to simulate a nuclear strike on the Twin Cities, the plane had been carrying six flight crewmembers and two instructors. The plane from the Sixty-Ninth Bomb Squadron, Forty-Second Bomb Wing of SAC, had departed Loring Air Force Base, Limestone, Maine, earlier in the day. It had made ECM runs at Bath, Maine; Albany, New York; Williamsport, Pennsylvania; and Youngstown and Bellefontaine, Ohio. The flight had continued to Richmond, Indiana, where a GPI Nav-bomb run was initiated that was to terminate at Minneapolis. There it would be scored for accuracy by the Air

Force Radar Bombing site at Wold-Chamberlain. Instead, seven of the crew members would not survive the training exercise.[44]

A memorial plaque at the crash site lists a dedication to the seven casualties:

On this spot on September 16, 1958 a U.S. Air Force B-52 bomber crashed while on a Cold War training mission originating from Loring Air Force Base, Limestone, Maine. Seven crew member gave their lives for their country. They were:

Captain Wm. Horstman, Pilot Kansas City, MO
Captain Richard J. Cantwell, navigator, Phoenix AZ
Major S.O. Gillespie, Jr., radar observer, Atlanta, GA
1st Lt Wm. F. Huskey, engineer, Norman, OK
T/Sgt. Leon R. Lew, tail gunner, Skokie, IL
Captain James D. Taylor, instructor, Dixon, KY
Captain Bernard D. Lanois, instructor, San Diego, CA

This marker has been erected in honor of the lost crewmen. Though from home far away and now long gone from this earth, they have not been forgotten by the citizens of Inver Grove Heights, the State of Minnesota, or the Country they so proudly served.

THE DAY A B-25 BOMBER CRASHED IN LEBANON, ILLINOIS

April 30, 1950, was shaping up to be another lazy, peaceful Sunday afternoon in this picturesque town when a B-25 bomber, having just taken off from Scott Air Force Base, nose-dived into a residential neighborhood and exploded.

The plane's six crewmen were all killed, four Lebanon residents were injured and a fifth went into shock and ten homes were damaged, one massively. Debris was scattered over a four-hundred-yard-long swath, and several human limbs were found in trees as far as a block away from the crash site, according to a report in the May 1 *Belleville News-Democrat*:

"When I saw the plane the first time, I don't believe it was more than 200 feet high," said Wilbert Beck, of 420 W. Schuetz St, whose horse suffered minor injuries when struck by debris. "It skimmed the buildings

on the north side of Dee Street as it came in from the northwest. Then it banked to the east and a tip of one wing cut a path through Wolf's living room. It hit the tree. Then came the explosion. Sheets of blue flames shot out in all directions. I ran behind my summer kitchen to escape injury from the wreckage. Once I looked up and saw a body sailing over my head."[45]

The Cold War Museum is dedicated to continuing education and preservation efforts of the era. To learn more or become involved, visit www.coldwar.org.

NOTES

Chapter 1

1. Encyclopedia of Chicago, "Red Squad," http://www.encyclopedia. chicagohistory.org/pages/1049.html.
2. Richard Dagger and Terence Ball, "Communism: Ideology," Encyclopedia Britannica, https://www.britannica.com/topic/communism.
3. People's World, "Charles E. Ruthenberg: The First Leader of the Communist Party USA," June 18, 2019, https://www.peoplesworld. org/article/charles-e-ruthenberg-the-first-leader-of-the-communist-party-usa.
4. Smithsonian National Postal Museum, "Chicago Bombs," https:// postalmuseum.si.edu/behindthebadge/chicago-bombs.html.
5. Christopher Sturdevant, *Cold War Wisconsin* (Charleston, SC: The History Press, 2018).

Chapter 2

6. Ronald Reagan, "Remarks at the Brandenburg Gate on June 12, 1987," American Rhetoric, https://americanrhetoric.com/speeches/ ronaldreaganbrandenburggate.htm.
7. Rick Perlstein, *The Invisible Bridge: The Fall of Nixon and the Rise of Reagan* (New York: Simon and Schuster, 2014).

8. Visit by the author to the Ronald Reagan birthplace in Dixon, Illinois.

9. Ronald Reagan, *An American Life* (New York: Simon & Schuster, 1990).

10. CommonLit, From "A Time for Choosing" Speech, 1964, https://www.commonlit.org/en/texts/from-a-time-for-choosing-speech.

11. Gene Kopelson, "50 Years Later: Ronald Reagan and North Korea's Hijacking of the USS *Pueblo*," *Washington Examiner*, January 23, 2018, https://www.washingtonexaminer.com/50-years-later-ronald-reagan-and-north-koreas-hijacking-of-theusspueblo.

12. Richard Rogala, USS *Pueblo* crew member detained in North Korea in 1968, conversations with the author.

13. Philip Klein, "Ronald Reagan Ripped the Soviet Cover-Up of Chernobyl," *Washington Examiner*, June 3, 2019, https://www.washingtonexaminer.com/opinion/ronald-reagan-ripped-the-soviet-cover-up-of-chernobyl.

14. *Los Angeles Times*, May 4, 1986.

15. Oliver North, *Under Fire: An American Story* (New York: HarperCollins, 1991).

Chapter 3

16. Andrew Feldman, *Ernesto: The Untold Story of Hemingway in Revolutionary Cuba* (New York: Melville House, 2019).

17. Abraham Lincoln Brigade Archives, http://www.alba-valb.org.

Chapter 4

18. Bible Gateway, https://www.biblegateway.com/passage/?search=Numbers+13&version=GW.

19. David Wise, *Spy: The Inside Story of How the FBI's Robert Hanssen Betrayed America* (New York: Random House, 2003).

20. As told to the author by Werner Juretzko.

21. Raymond Benson, interview by the author.

22. *Hollywood Reporter*, "Mila Kunis, Reese Witherspoon Sell Mystery Thrillers to ABC," https://www.hollywoodreporter.com/live-feed/mila-kunis-reese-witherspoon-sell-832250.

Chapter 5

23. FDR Library, "Einstein's Letter to President Franklin Delano

Roosevelt," August 2, 1939, http://www.fdrlibrary.marist.edu/archives/pdfs/docsworldwar.pdf.

24. Nuclear Illinois, NEIS (Nuclear Energy Information Service), http://neis.org/nuclear-illinois.

25. Victoria Sherrow, *The Making of the Atom Bomb* (n.p.: Lucent Books, 2000).

26. Nuclear Energy Institute, Illinois and Nuclear Energy Fact Sheet, https://www.nei.org/CorporateSite/media/filefolder/resources/fact-sheets/state-fact-sheets/Illinois-State-Fact-Sheet.pdf.

Chapter 6

27. Ed Thelen, locations of Nike missile sites, http://ed-thelen.org/loc-i.html.

Chapter 7

28. Wes Adamczyk, personal conversations with the author; Wesley Adamczyk, *When God Looked the Other Way: An Odyssey of War, Exile, and Redemption* (Chicago: University of Chicago Press, 2004).

29. *Chicago Tribune*, "Wesley Adamczyk, Author of Book on His Family's World War II Travails, Dies at 85," November 16, 2018, https://www.chicagotribune.com/news/obituaries/ct-met-wesley-adamczyk-obituary-20181113-story.html.

Chapter 8

30. David Edmonds, *Bobby Fischer Goes to War: How the Soviets Lost the Most Extraordinary Chess Match of All Time* (New York: HarperCollins, 2011).

Chapter 9

31. David Chudwin, "I Was a Teenage Space Reporter: From Apollo 11 to Our Future in Space" (n.p.: LID Publishing, April 2, 2019).

32. Marvin Rubenstein, *Apollo Memories: A Historical Look Back at the Early Days of Manned Spaceflight from the Viewpoint of a Chicago Teenager, in the Context of the Turbulent '60s* (n.p.: independently published, 2019).

Chapter 10

33. Space History, "Walt Disney and Wernher von Braun," https://www. space.com/15398-walt-disney-wernher-von-braun.html.

34. Mike Wright, "The Disney-Von Braun Collaboration and Its Influence on Space Exploration," Marshall Space Flight Center, NASA, https:// www.nasa.gov/centers/marshall/history/vonbraun/disney_article.html.

35. Quartzy, "The Propaganda Films that Saved Walt Disney's Cartoon Empire," https://qz.com/quartzy/1332008/the-propaganda-films-that-saved-walt-disneys-cartoon-empire.

Chapter 11

36. Fabián Escalante, *Executive Action: 634 Ways to Kill Fidel Castro* (Melbourne, AU: Ocean Press, 2006).

37. Thomas Maier, *Mafia Spies: The Inside Story of the CIA, Gangsters, JFK and Castro* (New York: Simon & Schuster, 2019).

Chapter 12

38. Scott Air Force Base, "History," https://www.scott.af.mil/About-Us/Fact-Sheets/Display/Article/159788/scott-air-force-base-history.

39. Naval Station Great Lakes, https://www.cnic.navy.mil/regions/cnrma/installations/ns_great_lakes.html.

40. Chanute Air Force Base, https://www2.illinois.gov/epa/topics/community-relations/sites/chanute-afb/Pages/default.aspx.

41. The Joliet Army Ammunition Plant, https://www.fs.usda.gov/detail/midewin/learning/history-culture/?cid=stelprdb5155180.

42. Rock Island Arsenal, https://www.army.mil/ria.

Chapter 13

43. Richard Reeves, *Daring Young Men: The Heroism and Triumph of The Berlin

Airlift, June 1948–May 1949, 1st ed. (New York: Simon & Schuster, 2010), 141.

44. "B-52 Crash, Inver Grove Heights, MN." Reprinted with permission from Noel Allard.

45. *Belleville News-Democrat*, "The Day a B25 Bomber Crashed in Lebanon," July 21, 2017, https://www.bnd.com/living/liv-columns-blogs/answer-man/article162829203.html.

INDEX

ABOUT THE AUTHOR

Christopher Sturdevant is a children's librarian who resides in Milwaukee, Wisconsin. His interest in the Cold War began while growing up during the 1980s. Chris studied history and physics at Carroll University. He is a U.S. Air Force veteran and chairman of the Midwest Chapter of the Cold War Museum in Washington, D.C. In addition, Chris has represented Team USA in masters-level track championships on three continents. His travels have taken him to North Korea, Chernobyl and Afghanistan.

Visit us at
www.historypress.com